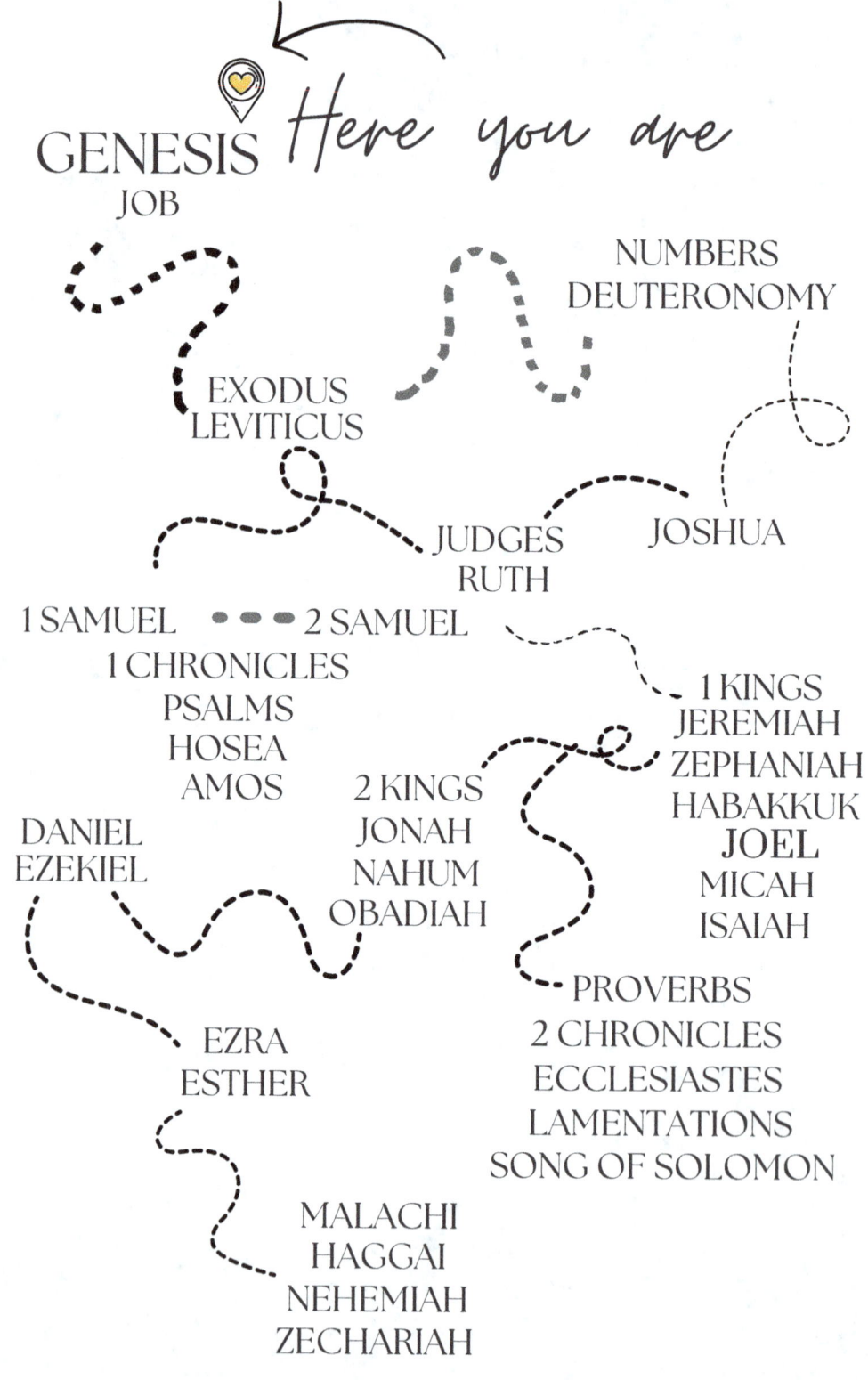

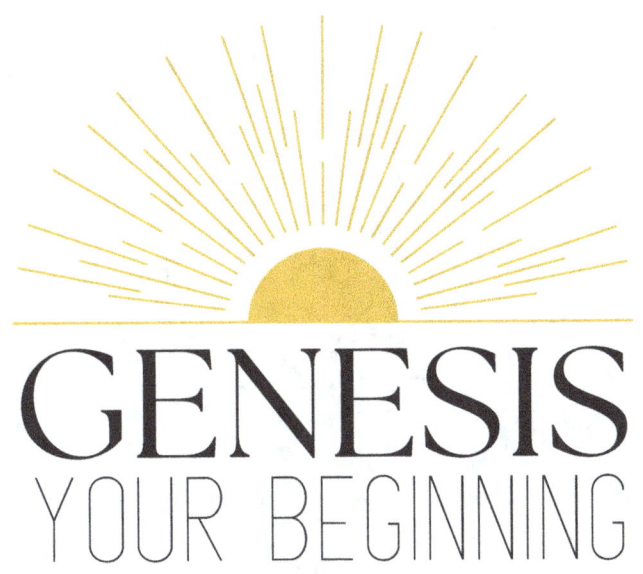

GENESIS
YOUR BEGINNING

Michelle Gautreaux

Genesis: Your Beginning
Lost & Found Bible Study Series
Published by United House Publishing
Concord, NC 28027
U.S.A.

Copyright © 2025 by Michelle Gautreaux
Published by *United House Publishing*

All rights reserved. Except for brief excerpts for review purposes, no part of this book may be reproduced or used in any form without written permission from the publisher.

All Scripture quotations are taken from the ESV* Bible
(The Holy Bible, English Standard Version*),
copyright 2025 by Michelle Gautreaux. All rights reserved.
The author has added italics for Scripture quotations for emphasis.

ISBN: 978-1-952840-59-3

Cover & Study© designed by Michelle Gautreaux in Canva

Printed in the United States of America
First Edition 2025

SPECIAL SALES
Most UNITED HOUSE books are available at special quantity discounts when purchased in bulk by corporations, organizations, and special-interest groups. For information, please e-mail orders@unitedhousepublishing.com

To my husband, Clint, who waited patiently for me to complete a story he always knew I would; to my son, Seth, who listened to each struggle I had with finding my story; to my son, Hunter, who gave me new ways of looking at my story; to my daughter, Claire, who, whether I liked it or not, gave me Godly wisdom in my story; and to the ladies in my Bible study (Amy, Ashley, Brandy, Charlene, Christine, Dinah, Katie, Kelly, Tammy, and Tracy) who took this story and turned it into theirs as they helped me put it all together.

Find Your Story

He knows your name.
He knows your pain.
He knows your joy.
And He knows your story.
Your story is His.

    Getting lost in what the Bible says isn't uncommon, but that doesn't mean it isn't for you. As you read about the men and women in the Bible, you will find messy stories full of turmoil, shame, and doubt, but what is ever-present is God's love and favor. What is lost in your story can be found in God's word. Find yourself in His story—God will not leave you lost in the wilderness - He will meet you right where you are.

    The Lost & Found Bible Study Series shares our connection to each book, chapter, and verse, not just in the Old or New Testament days, but what it means for us today. The Series consists of each book of the Bible as a Season, and each season is broken down into chapters as Episodes. You begin your journey at home with the Premiere by reading an Episode Trailer of the assigned chapters, and then you Read those chapters, taking notes and possible questions with the journal page given. Gathering with your group or alone in the Critique section, you will dig deeper with the Plug-In and break through any barriers with discussion questions in Discussion Bytes. We conclude the week with the Fan Club section by connecting Your Story to the chapters you have read and discussed by journaling at home. Then you are given a chance to get creative with your journaling by doodling and using any other type of art medium to express what God's word means to you in the Remix section. Finally, we end the session with Post Credits to the one and only, declaring His word over our lives daily with a prayer.

    As you hold this study in your hands, I pray for clarity in God's story for you. I pray you know you are loved and that God will continue to meet you where you are. You have a place in His story; every book, every chapter, and every verse is part of His story for YOU!

♡ *Michelle*

How this bible study works:

THE PREMIERE (PRE-SESSION):

 read the sneak peak of the assigned chapters to be read

 read assigned chapters and take notes or write questions

THE CRITIQUE (STUDY SESSION):

 read and discuss on your own or with your group

 answer questions and listen or watch podcast with study group (QR code on each page)

THE FAN CLUB (POST-SESSION):

 at home reflect on how your story connects to the chapters discussed

 a place to creatively express yourself as you connect to His word

 give credit where credit is due and declare this prayer over your life daily for the week ahead

GENESIS: YOUR BEGINNING
Season 1 • Lost & Found Bible Study Series • 2023 • Drama/Faith • 7 weeks

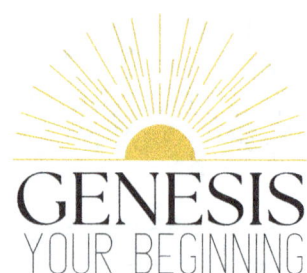

Starring: Adam, Eve, Noah, Abram, Sarai, Isaac, Jacob, Joseph ...

 WARNING: LOVE, VIOLENCE & TRUTH

Our beginning, read like the intro of a Star Wars film, would be, "In a heaven far, far away began the story of us . . ." Seriously, though, this book lays the foundation and groundwork for everything we read and experience in scripture. There is so much love and truth to be found in Genesis. Here begins the story of Jesus, but it is also the beginning of OUR story. We assume that because characters like Abraham and Noah have been written in the Bible, they knew God uniquely and made no mistakes. WRONG! Their story is written in the most sacred book, but that doesn't mean they were better, favored, or loved more. Their story is OUR story. The story of Jesus is OUR story.

All of humanity's brokenness begins in this book. We all have a Genesis chapter in our lives, a place where we begin, a place where we learn and grow, and a place of brokenness that brings us to God's promise. In Genesis, you will read some messed-up stuff, but what stands out is God's continuous grace, mercy, and determination to bless us all despite our actions. So, let's take the adventure and find YOUR story in the book of GENESIS!

genesis
1-7

EPISODE 1
Trailer

God's grand plan unfolds as He creates the world in seven days, starting the human race with Adam & Eve. Yet, like us, Eve was listening to those comments on her post again about what she should be eating while on her diet and then told her husband he needed to eat it, too (probably some pyramid scheme). Some punishments and grace were issued, kids were born, and sibling rivalry was taken too far. God told one of them, "You are punished, but I am gonna let you live" (I say that to my kids all the time). God said, "Let's hit that refresh button," and Adam & Eve have Seth, which eventually leads to Noah, the one man who could get this story rebooted. Noah's assignment: build a boat and put his family on it with food and supplies to survive the flood. Sounds easy enough. And he does (see, men can follow directions).

GENESIS 1-7

PLUG IN

THE plan

If we put together a crib with no instructions, we could skip a step, and the crib would not be deemed safe. God knew the plan for us had to be just right for it to work, so He carefully planned each day accordingly when He began His seven-day plan. He knew each step had its place, and each part was essential to the final product—no leftover screws in His plan.

His plan unfolds a little like this ...

"The earth was without form and void . . ." (1:2)

God filled the void and prepared the way. He has specifically planned the details of everything for you. But He also goes before you to fill a void you may not realize exists.

Day 1: Night & Day

"And God said, 'Let there be light,' . . ." (1:3)

There was first darkness, then light. There is so much hope in that discovery. With just a word from Him, the darkness you may feel you've succumbed to can be overcome.

Day 2: Sky

"And God made the expanse and separated the waters . . . And God called the expanse Heaven." (1:7-8)

Our God is so faithful; He never leaves us, but by separating Himself in this way, He patiently waits for us to seek Him.

Day 3: Land & Sea

". . . 'Let the water under the heavens be gathered together into one place, and let the dry land appear.'" (1:9)

In His carefully thought-out plan, God worked to supply our needs before we were placed on earth.

GENESIS 1-7

PLUG IN

THE plan

continued ...

Day 4: Sun, Moon & Stars
"... And let them be for signs and for seasons, ... and let them be lights in the expanse of the heavens to give light upon the earth.'" (1:14-15)

> We go through seasons of our lives: seasons of growth, humbleness, and even despair. Yet, even when darkness sets in, He created billions of light reminders that He is here in every season.

Day 5: Animals in the Sky & Sea
"And God said, 'Let the waters swarm with living creatures, and let birds fly above the earth ...'" (1:20)

> Preparing the Earth for us was a giant task. When I think of all the animals we have yet to discover, I wonder if the vast amounts of species were perhaps put on earth to prevent some of us from boredom.

Day 6: Animals on Land
"... 'and have dominion over' ..." (1:28)

> God respectfully placed us in the highest position on Earth. He laid out what He had provided and declared it enough for us.

Day 7: Rest
"So God blessed the seventh day and made it holy ..." (2:3)

> Knowing that God rests brings me reassurance that it is okay for us to rest as well. God declared this day holy, above all the other days.

GENESIS 1-7

PLUG IN

THE plan

continued ...

We can work our minds and bodies til nothing is left, and still, God recognizes the needed rest. How important our rest must be that He designated a whole day to it? Rest is not a part of my vocabulary, but it is the rest He declared in my life that led me to write this study. In the waiting, in the rest, I can respect the awe of it all.

His plan is never to forsake us but to bless us.

> "And God blessed them. And God said to them, "Be fruitful and multiply and fill the earth and subdue it . . ." (1:28)

When God said to be fruitful, multiply, fill the earth, and subdue it, He called forth a blessing for us to use the fruits of His spirit. His plan wasn't just for us to procreate but to overcome and fill the land with love, joy, peace, patience, kindness, goodness, faithfulness, gentleness, and self-control. Such a beautiful plan! One that looks better than any calendar full of pretty stickers. So, get those erasable pens out. His plan for you is already in motion.

GENESIS 1-7

PLUG IN

& EVE

Our first examples of the sinful nature and disobedience of mankind.

Before man labored in the field, God had provided for the land.

"and a mist was going up from the land and watering the whole face of the ground -" (2:6)

The Lord went before us to prepare the earth. Yet, He also made the land to provide for itself. There are times when we feel abandoned and empty as the earth before us, but could it be the Lord is teaching us what lies in us is already sufficient?

". . . then the Lord God formed the man of dust from the ground and breathed into his nostrils the breath of life, and the man became a living creature." (2:7)

The name Adam means humanity, and Eve means life. When we think of the word "humanity," compassion, brotherly love, and consideration also come to mind. God intentionally started the world with these ideas in mind. Adam and Eve were similar humans to us; they also struggled and succumbed to the devil's lies. This struggle reminds us of the importance of monitoring who we allow to speak into our lives and whom we should trust. Eve listened to what the serpent had to say about her, the tree, and God's word. The serpent caused her to doubt God's word for her.

". . . 'Did God actually say, "You shall not eat of any tree in the garden?"'" (3:1)

Adam & Eve

continued ...

When Satan causes us to doubt God's word, we try to micromanage His plan. In it, we become lost in what is meant for us. Adam and Eve decided what they had and who they were weren't enough. Sometimes, God keeps us from things because we are not yet ready or mature enough for them. Maybe Adam and Eve were not spiritually mature enough to handle the knowledge the tree contained. Not knowing what to do with the information after eating from the tree; they behaved inappropriately and sinfully. Adam and Eve made a sinful choice because they didn't trust the choice God made for them. They seized autonomy and defined good and evil for themselves. Do we pick the forbidden fruit over God's word? We see desirable things, and our flesh wants to convince us of their importance, where they can get us, or what they can get us.

After this sin came shame because when we know God, our hearts are convicted. Adam and Eve hid shamefully, and God called out for them. They had obtained the desirable thing they wanted but still felt empty and vulnerable. So they started playing the blame game, and God handled business.

"He said, 'Who told you that you were naked?'" (3:11)

He asked them who told them those lies (He wanted an address, y'all). What lies have you been fed? What forbidden fruit have you taken that wasn't meant for you? What fruit are we eating? God's word or someone's lies. And though Adam and Eve went against God's instructions, He didn't start by punishing them. He went straight to the root of the sin–the serpent–and cursed it.

PLUG IN

Adam & Eve

continued ...

    He declared some consequences to Adam & Eve but didn't shame them. He covered them with clothing better than they had chosen. His justice does not come after us but after the darkness that tried to attach itself to us. He gave them another chance and took them out of the garden, away from temptation. It is in our shame that we should go to Him; our brokenness can be healed in Him. We have to take ownership of our sins but not stay there. When sin entered the world, it broke the goodness of God's design but not His promise. I'm sure at this point, God was thinking I created this earth for you to live on, I gave you one rule to follow, and you couldn't get that right. As a parent, I can relate. Years ago, I prepared my home for the soon to be toddler in my home with outlet covers, corner bumpers and picked up all harmful things - explaining explicably that they must not be touched or to be careful. What I didn't bank on was the common misunderstanding of the human mind - curiosity. Though God creating us with it might be a bit of a conundrum it also has led to cures for diseases and progress for our world. So, why doesn't God remove us from every harmful situation and allows temptation? What we don't face, we can't overcome. We will never learn anything by removing what could harm us, hurt us, or cause us pain. For my toddler the outlet's intention was not meant to harm him, yet if mishandled, it would. The outlet is needed for electricity, but it is also required for the lesson. Therefore, we have to be adequately equipped to handle the lesson. Can we say our hearts are ready for the lesson?

1-7 GENESIS

PLUG IN

CAIN, ABEL & A MAN *named Noah*

Some follow directions, some don't - how's that working for us?

Typical sibling rivalry—yep, we all have probably been jealous of our siblings or someone close to us a time or two. Jealousy is like salt; too much can harm you. The climb to seeking another person's identity is a slippery slope. We can't be what God intended if we are too busy trying to be what He didn't intend. I don't think it was ever that Cain wasn't giving enough of his harvest and that Abel was giving more of his livestock. It was most likely how it was given.

> "In the course of time Cain brought to the Lord an offering of the fruit of the ground, and Abel also brought of the firstborn of his flock and of their fat portions. . . ."   (4:3-4)

You'll notice here it doesn't say that Abel brought his first offering with extra, yet Cain did not. Was the offering given with the Lord's glory in mind or his? Was he offering it out of duty instead of in faith? Cain checked the box; he did what he had to and thought it was enough. Abel gave from the top and then gave the overflow. He didn't fear the possibility of nothing being left; he just gave it all. Perhaps Cain wasn't convinced that God would multiply it if he gave it all. This reminds me of tithes. We regard it as a duty more than a way of worship, which could be why we don't see its fruit. Now, I am not saying we empty our bank accounts; let's be reasonable, but what if we gave from a place of the first and the extra? Not just in money but in time, love, and kindness. How could that change the world? God regarded Abel's offering above Cain's, and that caused Cain to be angry.

GENESIS 1-7

PLUG IN

CAIN, ABEL & A MAN *named Noah*

continued ...

So God tried to reason with Cain, giving him something to consider.

"The Lord said to Cain, 'Why are you angry, and why has your face fallen?' If you do well, will you not be accepted? And if you do not do well, sin is crouching at the door. Its desire is contrary to you, but you must rule over it." (4:6-7)

Cain harbored anger and resentment for the favor shown to Abel and slayed him. God cursed Cain, yet He spared his life.

Many people look at this story and focus on the curse God brought to his life. Yet, if Cain had viewed it as mercy, would some of his outcome and the generational curse that plagued his family have continued? God spared Cain's life and had mercy on him when He didn't deserve it. What are our decisions after God has grace and mercy on our lives?

Unto Adam & Eve came another son: Seth. This was their second chance at getting things right, which led to the lineage of Jesus. I named my oldest son Seth for this very reason. The short version of the story is that I wasn't making the best choices and needed a second chance from the Lord. He knew my actions against myself would end if I had another life to consider. This may not work for everyone, but it freed me from the bondage I put myself in.

Due to so much chaos, the world was calling out to the Lord. The Lord regretted all He had made and wanted to reboot humanity.

PLUG IN

CAIN, ABEL & A MAN
named Noah

continued ...

He saw the corruption and idolization in other men, so he sought a man who could lead Earth 2.0 and found Noah. Now everyone says, "AAAAWWW, Noah!" Noah was a man who, by standards of the Earth at the time, must have been like the kind older man down the street who cuts your lawn and brings your dog back when it gets off its leash. The world had disappointed God, and He was ready to start over.

"The Lord saw that the wickedness of man was great in the earth, and that every intention of the thoughts of his heart was only evil continually." (6:5)

So, God ordered Noah to build an ark with specific instructions, including who and what to take. He loaded the boat; it rained for forty days, the flood lasted for 150 days, and everything outside the ark and not within God's protection perished. How we respond determines the outcome we experience. We can't expect God's plan to work for us if we are not working on the plan. It doesn't always produce instant gratification, even when we work the plan out. I imagine Noah was scared that God's promise would never come as the days pressed on. Can you imagine being surrounded by water and having no end in sight? Maybe there was doubt in Noah's mind. Still, he stayed the course and waited for a move from God.

discussion BYTES

God created and prepared the earth before placing us on it. His carefully laid out plan included every provision we could ever imagine. What provisions has God given you that you didn't plan on needing?

_____
_____
_____

Eve's decision came from the input of a serpent, letting the lies influence her choice to take the forbidden fruit. Where in your life are you still choosing the forbidden fruit (the things you are not ready for or are not meant for you) over God's word? Are you allowing the input of others to change what God has for you?

_____
_____
_____

Abel's offering was given to glorify God, so he gave his best, whereas Cain gave out of duty. We can check all the boxes in our faith, but are we giving from the overflow or leftovers?

_____
_____
_____

The blueprint God had given Noah of how the ark was to be built was meticulous. God's plan for your life is designed in the same way. Sometimes, the plan can be long, challenging, and scary. Are you staying the course or abandoning the ship?

_____
_____
_____

PODCAST

1-7 GENESIS

How does your story connect now or in the past to Adam, Eve, Cain, Abel or Noah?

Sin broke the goodness but not the promise...

"THE LORD GOD MADE CLOTHING FROM SKINS FOR THE MAN AND HIS WIFE, AND HE CLOTHED THEM."
Genesis 3:21

POST Credits 🙌

Father,

I pray not to micromanage Your plan. I freely surrender my plan to You. You know exactly what I need, and I trust in You. When I interfere with your plan, let me be corrected. Lord, drive me out of the places I should not be as you did for Adam & Eve. I thank You in advance for Your mercy and grace for my actions and words that don't align with Your plan and word.

Amen

GENESIS 1-7

genesis
8-14

EPISODE 2
Trailer

In our previous episode, Noah & his people were on a boat with some smelly animals. The faucet was finally turned off, and Noah sent birds to confirm they could leave the Ark B&B and sustain life on the floating Earth 2.0. Their tour of Gilligan's Island would finally be over, and a beautiful sign of promise would be left. Noah would become caught up in a celebration gone wrong that involved his son. Afterward, some pent-up, attention-seeking humans would build a tower, and God would respond, "Negative, ghost rider" (Top Gun reference). Abram would enter the scene, and God would tell him to "pack it up and evacuate with ya girl." Abram would end up making the most irrational decisions by lying for some bread, but then, he would organize a successful rescue mission for his nephew after they parted ways.

8-14
GENESIS

8-14

GENESIS

PLUG IN

9048 HOUR tour

"God remembered Noah" (8:1). Did He really forget him? Our circumstances sometimes seem to drag on. We feel forgotten, but after our storms, we are promised rainbows.

Have you ever gone outside when it has been raining for days and wanted to crawl back into your house? I wonder how many days Noah and his family thought the same. Yet, with no other place to retreat, they remained on their boat and so continued the 9048-hour tour at sea. However, this wasn't one of those cruises where you are entertained by shows and bingo sessions. God caused a wind to pass over the earth, the water receded, and it stopped raining. The ark rested on the mountain of Ararat as the water continued to recede, and mountain tops became visible. Whether or not this timing was on purpose (because, yes, if you haven't caught on yet, I tend to overthink things), it leads me to think that this was a test of patience for the crew. Were they going to wait for God's sign or go out on their own accord?

Fortunately, they waited until that lovely dove we see all over bumper stickers brought back an olive leaf as a sign that life was indeed springing up. They stayed faithful with no word from God for almost over a year. I panic when I don't get confirmation weekly. Yet, Noah stayed faithful. I mean, honestly, did he have a choice? He could have jumped ship and been a man overboard, but would he have overcome his circumstances or been overcome by them?

"Then God said to Noah, 'Go out from the ark . . .'" (8:15-16)

What a relief! They finally get to check out of the Ark B&B. I would like to know the rating they would have given for that stay.

GENESIS 8-14

PLUG IN

9048 HOUR tour

continued ...

Noah showed gratitude to the Lord by building an altar and making burnt offerings. The Lord was pleased with the sweet aroma of prayers and said:

"... 'I will never again curse the ground because of man, for the intention of man's heart is evil from his youth. Neither will I ever again strike down every living creature as I have done.'" (8:21)

Thank you, Lord, but OUCH! "... the intention of man's heart is evil from youth." The Lord is well aware of how sinful we are. Though God knows that human nature may never change, He offers grace and mercy despite our sins. When we didn't deserve it, God gave us another chance. He rescues us from what we deserve, and because of Him, we are survivors of the storm.

God continued with His mission of Earth 2.0, instructing them to be fruitful and multiply while providing for all their needs. He established a few "life for a life" rules but ultimately reaffirmed His covenant with humanity through a rainbow in the sky.

"'I have set my bow in the cloud, and it shall be a sign of the covenant between me and the earth.'" (9:13)

God promised never to flood the earth again but never said we wouldn't face storms. Noah believed his work was done. I mean, he built an ark and had to live in it past its expiration date; that called for a break, right?

8-14 GENESIS

PLUG IN

9048 HOUR tour

continued ...

GENESIS 8-14

He planted a vineyard but got a little tipsy in the tent in only his birthday suit. Then his son, Ham, saw his dad unconsciously drunk and ran to tell his brothers, which led to him being cursed. Many interpretations have been given about this part of Genesis. What did Ham do to be cursed? Was there some shady action between Noah and Ham? One can maybe speculate that, but it seems pretty straightforward. He disrespected Noah and gossiped about his father's sin to his brothers. (Don't worry, we can pause here . . . I will give you and myself time to repent.) What an important lesson! Instead of doing as his brothers did to cover their father's sin and love him through it, Ham put it on display (insert a knife in the heart). We should not be putting our fellow brothers' and sisters' sins on display. It should be their testimony. Many times I have found myself in my anger about a situation and run to tell a friend about being wronged. I checked myself after reading this. Where was my heart when I ran to discuss this. Was it to vent or to shame the person? Lots of reflection. I tell my kids often "Check ya self, before ya wreck ya self."

Noah woke up the next day furious and cursed Ham but blessed Shem & Japheth. This led to nations we are familiar with. Shem's family, the nation of Israel; Japheth's family, the country north of Israel; and Ham's family, the ever-classy (insert sarcasm) Egyptians and Canaanites (enemies of Israel).

tower
OF BABEL

Here we go again on our own.

Are we really about to dedicate an entire page to nine verses of scripture in chapter eleven that only last five seconds? Of course, we are! In fact, we are going to make it three pages. There are some critical nuggets in this story explaining why God allows things to happen when they do. It was on purpose that God confused the people at the Tower of Babel, causing language barriers. The tower they were building was meant only to glorify them, not the Lord. God was protecting them from their demise. Someone once told me something that stuck with me for many years: It isn't rejection but God's protection. He was protecting them from themselves, not rejecting their gifts or them. He rejected the Tower of Babel because it would not bring about His promise and would lead to ill intentions. We get caught up in our feelings of rejection instead of looking at what God has for us or what He could be protecting us from. The bricks they used were a form of technology never seen before and became a trending topic. A topic that led to the desire to feel their recognition was more important than glorifying God.

"Then they said, 'Come, let us build ourselves a city and a tower with its top in the heavens, and let us make a name for ourselves, lest we be dispersed over the face of the whole earth.'" (11:4)

They weren't settling to be an average nation. They wanted their nation to be well known and not be lost among other nations.

GENESIS 8-14

PLUG IN

tower OF BABEL

continued ...

The Lord knew they intended to be greater than Him as they took pride in their work for the wrong reasons. We should be proud of our successes and achievements rather than vie for the attention that results. The light shining out of us should be greater than the light shining on us. Our gifts are given to us, and we should be humbled that the Lord chose us for them. Does that mean every gift is to be used in a ministry field for it to be considered glorifying God? No, but we should insert ourselves into the world with our gifts and show Jesus through our work.

The people who constructed the Tower of Babel were not united in honoring God but in sinning. The danger of a single person's sin is amplified when a large group is involved.

"And the Lord said, 'Behold, they are one people, and they have all one language, and this is only the beginning of what they will do. And nothing that they propose to do will now be impossible for them.'" (11:6)

Wars arise from sinful leadership. They create a new idea of what the world should be when we already have a guidebook with lessons the Lord teaches. God always has our best interest at heart. We think we know what is best for us, but confusion sets in if we don't fully surrender to what the Lord has for us. We can become confused by what is acceptable and what should be done in His will. He wants us to have our heart's desire, but not in a sinful manner.

GENESIS 8-14

PLUG IN

OF BABEL

continued ...

"Therefore its name was called Babel because there the Lord confused the language of all the earth. And from there the Lord dispersed them over the face of all the earth." (11:9)

    Having this distance and these language barriers might hinder us from many good things we could be doing together. In this instance, the good benefits outweighed the possible destructive consequences. The story could have looked very different had this tower and city flourished.

    Idolizing separates us from God; placing things before Him takes us away from His promises. Yes, sometimes it might look like there is some good in what we desire, yet a good thing isn't always a God thing. We might be disappointed in the separation from our desire, but what's behind door number two? What else does God have in store for us? What is He trying to set you apart for or from? Thank Him for His protection in what might feel like rejection.

8-14
GENESIS

PLUG IN

ABRAM & Sarai

The promise might not be for us to witness.

GENESIS 8-14

In chapter 12, we first see a family tree of a well-known couple in the Bible. If you haven't noticed the extensive family trees throughout Scripture, you will now. It is a foreshadowing of Jesus. Ever meet someone in your community and start asking who they are related to? Yeah, me too. (So, who's ya, mama?) In my younger days, it was to be sure I wasn't related to them and could date them. Though in these biblical times, they were all related, so there was no escaping that fact.

If we are familiar with the stories of this couple, it is easy to miss the details of where we can relate. The highlight reel with the cute pictures, posts, and updates of those leading that picture-perfect life can be misleading. This was Abram & Sarai. We could read the highlights and think, "Wow, Abram was such a faithful man and Sarai a beautiful woman," but then, as we dig deeper, we discover all the obstacles.

When the Lord called Abram to get his stuff, leave everything he had ever known, and go to where He would show him, He assured Abram he would be blessed. He didn't have AirBnB to look this up and check for that cute, one-of-a-kind, perfect place to stay along the journey. He went with no questions asked. The land of Ur was a beautiful area that I would be remiss to say was not easy to leave. They had been there a while and were very established. Yet, Abram obeyed and took his family with him, and then God made a promise to him.

"... 'To your offspring I will give this land.'" (12:7)

continued ...

Wait, rewind. Did God say to his offspring? Man, this is where you have to see how much faith Abram had. He had no offspring at the time, and the chances of this were slim at his age.

On the journey, Abram built an altar in appreciation, not for what was happening but for what would happen. This showed how much Abram honored his Father, but that didn't mean Abram wasn't capable of a little human error.

Upon entering Egypt, Abram lied about his wife. He feared what might be done to him having an older yet very attractive wife. He wasn't necessarily lying when he claimed she was related to him. Family trees were not pretty pictures hung up on mantles back then.

> "When he was about to enter Egypt, he said to Sarai his wife, 'I know that you are a woman beautiful in appearance, and when the Egyptians see you, they will say, 'This is his wife.' Then they will kill me, but they will let you live. Say you are my sister, that it may go well with me because of you, and that my life may be spared for your sake.'" (12:11-13)

Pharaoh was cursed for taking her, and this will be one of those questions I go to heaven with: Why? He obviously didn't know due to Abram's lie. Abram and Sarai are caught in the scheme. Pharaoh, upset by the betrayal, kicked them all to the curb.

GENESIS 8-14

ABRAM &

continued ...

"Why did you say, 'She is my sister,' so that I took her for my wife? Now then, here is your wife; take her, and go.' And Pharaoh gave men orders concerning him, and they sent him away with his wife and all that he had." (12:19-20)

Abram and his nephew were in discord throughout the journey out of Egypt. Finally, they peacefully decided to go separate ways, but Lot was imprisoned by the town he claimed as home. Abram then organized a rescue mission that led to the rescue of others and possessions that belonged to their allies.

"When Abram heard that his kinsman had been taken captive, he led forth his trained men, born in his house, 318 of them, and went in pursuit as far as Dan. And he divided his forces against them by night, he and his servants, and defeated them and pursued them to Hobah, north of Damascus." (14:14-15)

Despite Abram and Lot's issues with each other, they were placed aside to rescue Lot. Abram accepted nothing from the kings as a reward. Can we say we would do the same for our brothers and sisters even after discord?

discussion BYTES

Noah had much to consider for the year he was on the ark. He could have easily been overcome by his circumstances, but he overcame them by trusting God. Where in your life have you possibly been overcome by your circumstances?

_____
_____
_____
_____

The people of the land of Shinar were separated after they attempted to achieve fame from their tower. The tower of Babel became a trophy of their achievement. God was not happy, so he set them apart. What is God setting you apart from? Are you comfortable with it? How have you become comfortable with the separation?

_____
_____
_____
_____

After the discord between Abram and Lot, Abram still pursued helping his nephew Lot, planning a rescue mission to save him. What do you need to let go of to do the same? What do we hold on to that prevents us from operating as Christians, even in discord?

_____
_____
_____
_____

PODCAST

8-14

GENESIS

How does your story connect now or in the past to Noah and his sons, the people of Shinar or Abram and Sarai?

GENESIS 8-14

REMIX

Choosing His path over our own...

GENESIS 8-14

"THE LORD SAID TO ABRAM: GO FROM YOUR LAND, YOUR RELATIVES, AND YOUR FATHER'S HOUSE TO THE LAND THAT I WILL SHOW YOU."
Genesis 12:1

POST Credits

Father,

I cry out to You in my journey that Your will be done through my obedience, that my ideas of what I value begin with You. Chip away at this stony heart of mine, and despite discord, may I love others with intention, grace, and mercy, expecting nothing in return.

Amen

GENESIS 8-14

genesis
15-21

EPISODE 3
Trailer

In our last episode, Abram rescued Lot. The Lord told Abram he would have so many children running around his tent, he wouldn't be able to count them. (Lord, I don't want that; give that assignment to someone else.) Yet, their crib was empty. Abram & Sarai moved ahead on the assignment by involving their servant. (They didn't understand the assignment, y'all.) Baby Ishmael was born and wasn't the only one with a name change and circumcision. God got the last laugh and gave Abraham & Sarah their son, Isaac. Something terrible happened in the town next door, so Abe pleaded with God to rescue his family. He did, and some shady stuff started to go down—a little higher rating than PG-13 people.

15-21

GENESIS

15-21

GENESIS

PLUG IN

SARAI'S *infertility*

You are not the only one questioning and needing reminders.

So, now that Abram had led the rescue mission to get Lot, God reassured him His promise still stood.

"Fear not, Abram, I am your shield; your reward shall be very great." (15:1)

Great is our reward in heaven when we obey. He doesn't say when the reward will come; it is just that it is there. I am sure that is something we have all felt. I remember watching Back to the Future, and Doc said, "Don't tell me what happens because it will mess up the time combuliquiom" (whatever that word was). Do you think we would mess it up if we knew when a promise was to come? I believe God keeps some of it from us so we don't make decisions that could affect the outcome. Abram, unconvinced, questioned God (see, we are not the only ones) and worried that the promise of children would never come to pass. Then God was like, Abram - do you know who I am? I said, do you know who I am? Still unconvinced, God asked Abram for some crazy requests in sacrifices.

15-21 GENESIS

"He said to him, 'Bring me a heifer three years old, a female goat three years old, a ram three years old, a turtledove, and a young pigeon.' And he brought him all these, cut them in half, and laid each half over against the other. But he did not cut the birds in half." (15:9-10)

If you dig deeper, you can find plenty of meaning to all these sacrifice requests. The sole purpose of this covenant was the fertility of Abram's wife.

PLUG IN

SARAI'S *infertility* continued ...

For Jews, a dove symbolized fertility and the spirit of God, so it would not be cut open. Two of the sacrifices were females representing Sarai, and the third meant completeness and stability. The age of the animals brought reassurance the promise would be fulfilled. Finally, the cutting was a blood covenant to seal the deal. While Abram was asleep, he had a nightmare, and the Lord was persistent with Abram. God gave Abram a timeline showing him his people would live like slaves for 400 years, but not to worry, they would prosper. (Well, thank goodness. That 400 years a slave looked rough.)

But alas, God shared with Abram he would never see the promise. You might not see the fruit of your labor on this side of heaven. I can't say I blame Abram for being reminded to persevere. I can't even wait 400 seconds, much less 400 years. And it wasn't like he was saying Abram would get it personally; it was for his offspring. That's like dangling a jelly-filled donut with oozing icing in front of your face and saying, "See this, it ain't for you, but good news, you can look at it, and I will give it to your kin." Talk about some self-control there, but don't worry, we are not the only ones breaking the diet-—cough, cough—Sarai & Abram. The scale never lies. When things are not happening on our timeline, we tend to take matters into our own hands.

Abram & Sarai became doubtful and tried to fulfill God's promise independently. How many times have we been there, only to discover that had we waited a bit longer, the promise was around the corner?

GENESIS 15-21

PLUG IN

SARAI'S *infertility*

continued ...

Sarai doubted God's promise and tried to micromanage the plan by offering their servant as plan B. Yet, Hagar becoming pregnant made Sarai mad. Maybe Sarai thought Abram would never go through with it? Was it a test? Abram then handed the problem off to Sarai. (From now on, men, nothing you ever do will be right - sorry, I will pray for you.)

I have sympathy for Hagar being thrown right in the middle of a married couple's struggle with infertility, but did she have a choice in the matter? Could she have refused? Hagar fled following Sarai's confrontation, but an angel of the Lord went after her.

> "And the angel of the Lord said to her, 'Behold, you are pregnant and shall bear a son. You shall call his name Ishmael, because the Lord has listened to your affliction.'" (16:11)

How beautiful is it that the Lord would still go after her despite what she had done? He heard her cries in the wilderness and came to her. He meets us where we are.

> "'He shall be a wild donkey of a man, his hand against everyone and everyone's hand against him, and he shall dwell over against all his kinsmen.'" (16:12)

Cue palm smack to forehead. Hagar was probably thinking, "Great, I get a wild donkey," and thus was born Ishmael.

GENESIS 15-21

PLUG IN

ABRAM TO Abraham

Time for a name change; we have things to do.

Abram realized he had fallen again. There is no witness protection program here, but a name change happened to both Abram (great-father) & Sarai (my princess), and they became Abraham (father of multitudes) & Sarah (a princess). God never said we would not see hurts in the world but that we are made new in Him. I believe this name change was meant to be a fresh start and a covenant to whom God labeled them to be, not what society had labeled them. So God then asked,

> "every male among you shall be circumcised. You shall be circumcised in the flesh of your foreskins, and it shall be a sign of the covenant between me and you." (17:10-11)

Oy! Hard pass, right? Circumcision was not done as a baby. This is the first mention of it, and in researching it, this display of cutting was a way of cutting the sinfulness of our flesh off. Remember those sacrifices earlier? Here, again, was another blood covenant sealed between man and God. These obedient men of God did as told, and then the Lord again gave Abraham the promise of a child to be born of Sarah.

> "Then Abraham fell on his face and laughed . . ." (17:17)

Abraham, ROFL, literally, see, I can't make this up. He was laughing because, in his flesh, he didn't see how this was possible.

15-21 GENESIS

PLUG IN

ABRAM TO
Abraham

continued ...

Sarah was barren, and they were too old to be first-time parents. Then God, being the jokester He is, said to Abraham, because you laughed, you will name him Isaac, meaning laughter. Three angels visited Abraham and repeated the promise of a child with a deadline.

"The Lord said, 'I will surely return to you about this time next year, and Sarah your wife shall have a son.' ..." (18:10)

Sarah overheard the conversation and laughed. Securing that namesake, are we Sarah? In embarrassment, she denied it, and the Lord called her out: Umm, no, you did laugh.

We can deny the works of God or line up with them. The plan could be the most ridiculous, impossible, and implausible plan you have ever heard. But with God at the helm, nothing could be more entertaining than watching it all play out. You will face-plant right into where He planned all along, and He'll have the last laugh. The absurdity of it all will surprise you, leaving you dumbfounded and joyful. And the laughter you once had in denial of the possibility will be the same but with the joy of the possibility.

Looking at me now, my pre-Jesus life would be a tale you would most likely never believe. Those who knew me then would probably laugh at the thought of me writing a Bible study. It would be quite humorous to you if I told you all of the strange happenings of my life. Some of the stories might even seem fictional. I am not hiding the darkness, but I don't live in it.

PLUG IN

ABRAM TO Abraham

continued ...

The past is the past: I've learned, I've grown, and I still need to work out a few kinks. BUT to stay there is not an option for me. My name change comes with a reputation, perspective, and spiritual change I am forever grateful for. That isn't to say the old me doesn't creep around the corner when I get very passionate about something, but I know where my truth is kept. I return to that every time instead of the bottom of the pit where I once lay.

The plans God has placed before me are ones I would never have put in my planner years ago. I would have never fathomed them and, therefore, would have never written something I felt ill-equipped to write. Yet, here I am writing what I hope to be the first of many studies that will have others thinking about their story in God's book.

We are created in His image, and He places within us His strength. We underestimate God when we underestimate His creation. When we look at ourselves as mistakes and full of impossibility, then we insult our creator. He doesn't make mistakes and makes impossible things happen—so why not Abraham & Sarah? Why not me? Why not YOU?

GENESIS 15-21

PLUG IN

pillar OF SALT

Our faith reduced to a pillar of salt.

The Lord saw yet another town up to no good and intervened. Abraham felt a little brave with his newfound name and asked the Lord to save the righteous. He started with fifty and then continued down to ten. The fact that Abraham kept pushing didn't come as a surprise to the Lord. He knew the true lesson for Abraham was how far he would go to save the righteous and whether he would be brave enough for the task. Abraham proved he was by asking the Lord for favor over a city that might not have seemed worthy.

So the angels went to Sodom and came upon Lot. Lot saw them and begged them to stay in his home, so he could serve them. While there, men in the town heard about Lot's guests and came to take them out for a night on the town (it was worse than that—I'm just trying to keep it PG, okay!). So, Lot offered up his daughters to the men of the town—explain yourself, Lot! Yet, the men were unsatisfied with that compelling offer and pushed their way into the house, only to scramble around blinded by the angels. The angels told Lot to get out of town with his family because the Lord was about to bring the hammer down on this place of wicked people. His sons-in-law thought he was joking and stayed as Lot left town with his wife and two daughters.

"And as they brought them out, one said, 'Escape for your life. Do not look back or stop anywhere in the valley. Escape to the hills, lest you be swept away.'" (19:17)

PLUG IN

pillar OF SALT

continued ...

 Grateful for the chance to leave, Lot thanked them but asked to go to a different town. As they escaped, Lot's wife looked back and turned into a pillar of salt. Have mercy (said in my best Uncle Jesse voice)! How many of us have looked back, though, at what once was the destruction of our lives and stayed stuck: stuck in our sin, grief, or bitterness? We can't fault her. We have all done it, but God has mercy on us. Thankfully, we do not all turn into pillars of salt here but are asked to be the salt of the earth.

 God then invited Abraham to see what He had done for him. Lot had come out of the destruction

 (cue smoke machines and a large explosion behind Lot).

PLUG IN

Unlikely BIRTH

Regardless of our actions, the Lord's promise will be fulfulled.

Lot asked for his family to go to another town instead of the one the Lord called him to inhabit. Well, guess what? He lived in fear in the city he requested. See how that works? God will listen to our requests, but He also wants us to learn lessons when we don't trust His word for our lives. Lot and his daughters resorted to living in a cave; the daughters wanted children so badly that they got Lot drunk, and both became pregnant. (I know, this is becoming a bad episode of Jerry Springer.) They backslid to the sins of their former city. Yet, in it, we discover these births led to two tribes in history that would explain much of what we are going through now—the Moabites and the Ammonites. These tribes were born with a generational curse lasting hundreds of years.

In another journey of Abraham, a similar story was played out. Abraham told another half-truth about his wife to protect himself from the King of Gerar, Abimelech. It is disappointing that, once again, Abraham disregarded the curses that could be brought to those he encountered due to his lie. Out of fear, like Abraham, we can make rash decisions and repeat them often. Abimelech was astounded by a dream he had about Sarah and pleaded with the Lord.

"... So he said, 'Lord, will you kill an innocent people? Did he not himself say to me, 'She is my sister'? And she herself said, 'He is my brother.'..." (20:4-5)

GENESIS 15-21

PLUG IN

Unlikely BIRTH

continued ...

The Lord showed mercy to Abimelech and told him to return Sarah, for Abraham was a prophet. God uses the most unlikely, even those who mess up, to carry out His plan. After hearing Abraham's fear, Abimelech had mercy and grace on Abraham, blessing him with livestock and land. He forgave him, and Abraham prayed for Abimelech—so beautiful!

Finally, Sarah gave birth to Isaac, as God promised. Abraham was at the ripe old age of 100, and Sarah was ninety years young when Isaac was born. However, this wasn't unusual if you look back on their ancestors. It wasn't the age that was a big deal. It was the fact that she had been barren for many years. The thought of ever having children had become a far-fetched idea. Now that Sarah had the promise they had been waiting on, she wanted Hagar and Ishmael gone.

Ishmael bullied his younger brother, and this "mama drama" became too much for Abraham.

> "But God said to Abraham, 'Be not displeased because of the boy and because of your slave woman. Whatever Sarah says to you, do as she tells you, for through Isaac shall your offspring be named. And I will make a nation of the son of the slave woman also, because he is your offspring.'" (21:12-13)

Hagar and Ishmael went into the wilderness again. Close to dehydration and starvation, Hagar cried out to the Lord.

GENESIS 15-21

PLUG IN

Unlikely BIRTH

continued ...

She wept, asking not to see the death of her son. Should we ever find ourselves in the wilderness, which we will, may we always cry out as Hagar did.

"'What troubles you, Hagar? Fear not, for God has heard the voice of the boy where he is. Up! Lift up the boy, and hold him fast with your hand, for I will make him into a great nation.'"
(21:17-18)

(cue The Lion King scene)

Our lives will remain a wilderness we will never overcome if we don't surrender ourselves to Him.

God then provided Hagar and Ishmael a well, and they drank out of it. That great nation He spoke of is the Arab nation, and Isaac's would be the Jewish nation.

Abimelech was back in the picture. Recognizing that God blessed Abraham, he wanted him as an ally. Yet, due to the former betrayal, he asked for a treaty to be drawn up. Good thinking, Abimelech!

At the end of this chapter, Abraham planted a tree as a sign of his commitment to being rooted in God's promise and living in a land where he wasn't comfortable.

"Abraham planted a tamarisk tree in Beersheba and called there on the name of the Lord, the Everlasting God. And Abraham sojourned many days in the land of the Philistines." (21:33-34)

discussion BYTES

We can grow weary when we don't see the promises of the Lord fulfilled. God's timing feels years away. Abram & Sarai waited for what seemed to be an eternity for their promised child. What has resulted from trying to fulfill God's promise in your life before His timing? Or, what have you learned in the delay?

_____
_____
_____

Lot's wife had so much to look forward to in the new place God was leading them. God had spared them. What caused her to pause and look back? We can get stuck when we are unwilling to leave little pieces of our lives behind. What has been difficult to let go of and prevented you from moving forward? Where are you stuck? Or have you managed to move forward after a difficult time in your life, leaning on the future and not the past?

_____
_____
_____

Hagar bore her soul in the wilderness as she cried out to the Lord for her son. Her desperate cries to Him received the Lord's attention. In your moment of despair, what are your actions? Are you crying out to the Lord or trying to fix it yourself?

_____
_____
_____

PODCAST

GENESIS 15-21

How does your story connect now or in the past to Abraham and Sarah, Hagar or Lot and his wife?

Out of the wilderness comes greatness...

15-21

"GET UP, HELP THE BOY UP, AND GRASP HIS HAND, FOR I WILL MAKE HIM A GREAT NATION."
Genesis 21:18

POST Credits 🙌

Father,

I come humbly to You, crying out of the wilderness for freedom from the shackles I have placed on my own life—the weights I have added to my own imprisonment and the times I have taken matters into my own hands only to block Your blessings and Your promises. I repent and ask that I am open to the reminders You send to see Your promises through.

Amen

GENESIS 15-21

EPISODE 4
Trailer

Coming up on As Abraham's World Turns, Abraham is faced with a sacrifice that would make any parent shudder. God was like, "Hey, you know that kid I promised you? Well, you're gonna have to give him back now." God asked Abraham to sacrifice Isaac, and without hesitation, Abe followed orders. But wait. Plot twist . . . God sent him the sacrifice needed. An unusual oath ritual took place. Then, Isaac is blessed with a wife from the homeland, and they have twins. One gets hangry, giving up his birthright for a bowl of stew, but that won't be all Esau loses by the end of these chapters. Jacob has to leave, and on his journey, he has a dream . . .

22-28
GENESIS

22-28

GENESIS

PLUG IN

A HARD *Sacrifice*

Here is where it starts to get real! (who am I kidding? I think I say that in every chapter.)

> "After these things God tested Abraham and said to him, 'Abraham!' And he said, 'Here I am.' He said, 'Take your son, your only son Isaac, whom you love, and go to the land of Moriah, and offer him there as a burnt offering on one of the mountains of which I shall tell you.'" (22:1-2)

Have you ever prepared for a test and thought, "I got this!" Then, when test day finally comes, you begin to spaz out. You think I should know all the answers to this test, but I am still panicking. Years ago, I was nervous about a science test, so I took the study guide and copied the whole thing on one sheet of paper to cheat (sorry, Mr. Allemand). Then, feeling like I would get caught, I copied it again, this time on a half sheet. Still, I was sweating, so I copied it to a quarter sheet, and as I did, I shortened and abbreviated the notes. That quarter sheet glared at me, so I again reduced its size to an eighth, summarizing and abbreviating it all again. At this point, I thought surely he wouldn't see me looking at this cheat sheet. When I got to my class for the test, I didn't look at that paper once. I knew everything on it.

Can we say, without a doubt, that we have walked with God repeatedly and memorized what it feels like to trust Him? Abraham surely did. When God asked Abraham to sacrifice the son He had just given him, Abraham wasn't nervous about this major test. He knew what it was like to walk with God and would not need to cheat his way through it. He had witnessed God's work before, and though difficult, he had faith that a provision would be made.

GENESIS 22-28

PLUG IN

A HARD *Sacrifice*

continued...

    Abraham took his now-grown son and two young men on the journey. He asked that the young men stay behind at the foot of the mountain. He proceeded with Isaac up the mountain giving him the wood to carry. Our Savior would carry the wood to a sacrifice in the same area hundreds of years later. Can you imagine what Abraham's son was thinking? I mean, this sounds like one of those crime documentaries that my children get tired of me watching.

    Isaac let his dad bind him and asked his dad where the lamb was for the burnt offering. It's you, Isaac, you are the sacrifice . . . until God intervened by sending an Angel with provisions.

> "And Abraham lifted up his eyes and looked, and behold, behind him was a ram, caught in a thicket by his horns. And Abraham went and took the ram and offered it up as a burnt offering instead of his son." (22:13)

    Whew! That was close! Abe named the mount "The Lord Will Provide," and the angel of the Lord confirmed God's promises to him. He told him it was because he obeyed that the promise would be fulfilled. It isn't that God's promises are not there waiting for us, but we walk away from them by our choices. Out of our obedience flows provision and blessings. The promises stood on Isaac staying alive—the promise of descendants that outnumber the stars. Abraham knew this, so his fear was not in losing Isaac but in not obeying.

GENESIS 22-28

PLUG IN

A HARD Sacrifice

continued ...

"'and in your offspring shall all the nations of the earth be blessed, because you have obeyed my voice.'" (22:18)

Several times throughout the Bible, the Lord asks, "Where are you?" and many hide in shame. Yet, the response from Abraham is always, "Here I am." Our blessings are based on our response and willingness to be where God intends. Despite our circumstances or sins, our willingness to stand on His rock shows our faithfulness to Him. We can't hide from Him when we make mistakes, for it is in our mistakes that God does His greatest work. We must declare our faith by response—Here I am, Lord. Here—I—am.

An extended family tree is listed at the end of the chapter, but its importance is merely genealogical. It is to familiarize you with the people in these stories. These family trees can feel cumbersome, but each has a purpose. This example is of Abe's brother Nahor. He has twelve sons, one of them being Bethuel, the father of Rebekah, whom we will discuss soon.

PLUG IN

posture OF OUR HEART

A dying man's request: just marry a good woman (and all the boy moms say amen!)

Twenty years later, Sarah died. Abraham and Sarah didn't own a family burial plot, so he had to request one. Abe must have been a well-known man of faith because the community offered their finest burial place, the cave of Machpelah, which belonged to Noah's grandson, Ephron. The field and cave were offered for free, but Abraham paid 400 shekels of silver ($120+). Abraham then buried Sarah there.

Many years later, Abraham asked his servant to find a suitable bride for Isaac from their homeland. He made what seemed to be an unusual oath ritual, asking the servant to put his hand "under his [Abraham's] thigh." It was culturally appropriate, at the time, to do this, demonstrating submission to authority and obedience to the person asking the favor. Abraham agreed if the servant could not find a wife willing to come for Isaac, he would be free of the oath. The faithful servant committed to the trip and prayed along the way,

"And he said, 'O Lord, God of my master Abraham, please grant me success today and show steadfast love to my master Abraham.'" (24:12)

He placed himself at a well where all the townsmen's daughters drew up water. Interestingly, the servant's prayer was one of respect for his master. He requested that the woman be one of kindness, generosity, and compassion in an offer to give the servant and his camels a drink. It is believed that this servant is the servant mentioned in 15:2.

22-28 GENESIS

PLUG IN

posture OF OUR HEART

continued ...

He was the servant who would be the potential heir of Abraham's house. His respect and care for his master earned him the same respect in return.

Behold, Rebekah—the woman he had just finished praying for. She checked off all the boxes. The servant placed bracelets on her wrists and a ring on her nose. Quite an unusual way to claim a wife, right? Yet, this was the culture of the Middle East to induce submissiveness, laying claim to the person they had chosen. This was always a challenge for me to understand when spoken about in the Bible. Being submissive felt like someone would be given power and control over me, something I struggled with because of the pain and hurt I had experienced from many who tried to control me. Being submissive meant conforming to what others said, and that wasn't exactly easy for me—I had trust issues.

Conforming in the biblical sense means validating and trusting the other person in the decision-making. Not exactly the easiest thing to do when we naturally want to be right in every situation. I still have some work to do in this area, so thankfully, God has grace and mercy on me when I want to declare my win, paint my body green and gold, and do a victory dance in the streets. I tell ya, God has His hands full with me.

What the servant did next was so special. He took a moment to worship the Lord.

GENESIS 22-28

PLUG IN

posture
OF OUR HEART

continued ...

"The man bowed his head and worshiped the Lord and said, 'Blessed be the Lord, the God of my master Abraham, who has not forsaken his steadfast love and his faithfulness toward my master. As for me, the Lord has led me in the way to the house of my master's kinsmen.'" (24:26-27)

Such a beautiful moment. He took the time to worship and thank the Lord right there, in that very moment. He paused to appreciate all the Lord had provided.

Rebekah ran home to tell her family about her new flame, and her brother, Laban, ran out to the well and invited the servant and his men to their home and prepared a place for them to stay along with the camels. The servant accepted and was taken care of by the family. He paused before eating the feast laid before them and explained his purpose for the journey. He told of Abraham's riches and blessings from the Lord and that Abe's son, Isaac, was just as blessed. The servant then shared his oath with his master and his prayer at the well. Read that again! He shared his testimony of faith. We often overlook sharing this and only share the significant testimonies in life—the life-changing, miracle-working ones. If we took time to glorify Him in the little things, we would create a daily habit of doing so. Finally, the servant laid out his master's requests, and surprisingly, the family agreed, recognizing the Lord's hands in it.

"Then Laban and Bethuel answered and said, 'The thing has come from the Lord; we cannot speak to you bad or good.'" (24:50)

22-28 GENESIS

PLUG IN

posture OF OUR HEART

continued ...

Rebekah was granted permission to go, the servant worshiped the Lord, and gifts were showered on Rebekah and her family. They rested for the night but had second thoughts in the morning. Maybe some pre-empty nest feelings, but they asked for just ten more days.

The servant pleaded for them not to delay him or the hand of God. The key thing that this servant recognized was that their disobedience could delay but not stop the hand of God. So, the parents called in their daughter for consent. Rebekah had to consent; Jewish practices were clear on this. She agreed to go with the servant but took along her nurse, Deborah, who had cared for her since birth. Deborah was what we would call a nanny today. Rebekah was then blessed and sent on her way.

"And Isaac went out to meditate in the field toward evening. And he lifted up his eyes and saw, and behold, there were camels coming. And Rebekah lifted up her eyes, and when she saw Isaac, she dismounted from the camel and said to the servant, 'Who is that man, walking in the field to meet us?' ..." (24:63-65)

GENESIS 22-28

Move over Ryan Gosling; here comes Isaac. This is exactly how my husband and I met; add a few pool tables, and you get the picture. Isaac immediately fell in love with her—mind you, without seeing her face—and took her as his wife.

PLUG IN

posture
OF OUR HEART

continued ...

    Now that Sarah was gone, Abraham married another wife named Keturah, and they had many children. ({shoulder shrug} He was told he would have as many descendants as stars in the sky). Abe gave it all to Isaac and blessed his other sons with gifts. Abraham then died at 175 and was buried alongside Sarah. Ishmael and Isaac united to bury their father, which is so encouraging despite all the rivalry they once had.

    ROLL CALL . . . Ishmael? . . . Here. Nebaioth? . . . Here. Kedar? . . . Here. Adbeel? . . . Here. I have been a teacher before, and I will tell you, I would not have pronounced a single name on this roll call correctly. This family tree becomes extensive, but remember, when Ishmael was born, God said he would bless him with twelve tribes. Here they are—the twelve tribes He promised Hagar. In Assyria, near his family, Ishmael died at the age of 137.

GENESIS 22-28

PLUG IN

OVER A *bowl* OF STEW

At least here in Louisiana, we're not trading for anything less than a bowl of gumbo.

GENESIS 22-28

Still in the honeymoon phase, Rebekah and Isaac wanted children. So Isaac prayed on behalf of his wife, and God blessed her with not one but two children. If any of you have been pregnant, you most likely remember your baby moving in your belly. Imagine two wrestling in there.

> "And the Lord said to her, 'Two nations are in your womb, and two peoples from within you shall be divided; the one shall be stronger than the other, the older shall serve the younger.'" (25:23)

If you thought the sibling rivalry between Cain and Abel was challenging to read, prepare for the story of Esau and Jacob. These boys were opposites indeed. Jacob grabbed his brother's heel at birth, labeling him as the "heel grabber and deceiver." What we learn is that quite often, Jacob would repeat this pattern. Are the habitual things we gravitate to becoming a pattern in our lives that might be causing harm?

According to the culture at this time, since Esau was born first, he was to receive the birthright. That meant he would receive twice his brother's inheritance. Jacob was a homebody, a mama's boy, similar to Forrest Gump. I would compare Esau, the outdoor manly man, to Gaston from Beauty and the Beast since Gaston hunted like Esau. Or maybe Esau was more like the Beast—they both were some hairy dudes.

PLUG IN

OVER A *bowl* OF STEW

continued ...

Esau came home one day starving, and Jacob offered him some stew in exchange for his birthright. Yes, you heard that right. He gave up his inheritance for some stew. Who does that? Esau does! It's okay, Esau; my husband might have done the same. Have we sold our inheritance because we thought it wasn't worth it, deserved, or needed, believing the sin would be better than the blessing ahead?

Famine struck again, so Isaac and Rebekah left and ended up in Gerar as God requested. They, like Abraham, had to stay in a land that was foreign to them. Something truly uncomfortable for most of us is staying where we feel like "aliens," a place where we know no one or doesn't bring contentment. We shouldn't be asking for comfort. Instead we should be asking, what is God building in us while in unfamiliar territory?

Like his father, Isaac tried to pass off Rebekah as his sister. But Abimelech (different one from his father's similar situation) caught them together, called out Isaac, and then ordered all the males in the country not to touch her, or they would be put to death.

Isaac became rich in the land, was seen as a threat, and was asked to leave. When he left, he camped where his father had camped before and dug up his father's filled-in wells. Some village people became jealous of the spring waters discovered and laid claim to it.

GENESIS 22-28

 OF STEW

continued ...

Isaac's faith that the Lord would continue to provide was rooted in his perseverance in digging one well after another and not quarreling with the village people over whose real estate it was. He was confident God would continue providing a spring water well. And through his confidence and faith, the Lord provided. The provision was made by his faith. Isaac didn't spend days worrying about where they would get water, only trusting some would be at the next well. There could be a whole sermon made for me on this one part of scripture. Had I just kept moving forward knowing it was already taken care of maybe I wouldn't have wasted so many days worrying.

"And he moved from there and dug another well, and they did not quarrel over it. So he called its name Rehoboth, saying 'For now the Lord has made room for us, and we shall be fruitful in the land.'" (26:22)

The Lord reconfirmed to Isaac the promises He made to Abraham, and Isaac built an altar. Abimelech heard of Isaac's glorious blessings and presented a proposal to Isaac, who peacefully agreed and exchanged oaths over a meal. Abimelech wanted to align with Isaac's blessings, hoping to get a bit for himself.

GENESIS 22-28

PLUG IN

Yoked TO WHAT

Can we all just get along?

Esau had two wives and didn't make life easy for his parents. Isaac, partially blind, asked Esau to hunt and prepare a last meal for him. Rebekah heard this and convinced Jacob to grab their goats, so she could prepare the meal. She wanted her favorite child to receive the blessing instead of Esau. Jacob was doubtful and worried he would be cursed if the trick did not work. Jacob was not worried about the morality of the lie but only the curse he would receive from it. It was not considered that the apparent difference in who hit puberty first might thwart the plan. Yet, good ol' Mama had an idea. She told him, "Don't worry, the curse will be on me." The plan was put into action. Jacob entered under the guise of his brother with goat skins on his arms and food in his hands. The plan worked, and Jacob was blessed. Esau returned from his hunt unaware, prepared the food, brought it to his father, and asked for his blessing. Isaac was confused and then realized he had been tricked. Esau was furious and asked that he, too, be blessed. Yet, Isaac told him Jacob had taken that blessing. Esau asked for at least one blessing, but it came with some stipulations. Isaac told him life wouldn't be easy, and he would carry these burdens until he could forgive his brother.

"'By your sword you shall live, and you shall serve your brother; but when you grow restless you shall break his yoke from your neck.'" (27:40)

GENESIS 22-28

PLUG IN

Yoked to What

continued ...

Esau wasn't hearing it. Oh, what a lesson here in forgiveness. We carry the yoke of bitterness and anger when someone has sinned against us. This is not an easy lesson to learn. I realized early on if I held myself in bondage by others' sins I was only harming myself - forgiveness was key to my freedom and healing.

Esau was not so convinced that forgiveness be his course of action. He swore to kill Jacob, and this concerned Rebekah. She asked that Jacob live with her brother Laban until Esau cooled off. He left with a blessing and was told to marry a woman from the homeland. Esau took another wife, Ishmael's daughter, thinking he could gain favor but he did not. The last thing to happen in this chapter: Jacob had a dream on his journey to Laban's house of a ladder where angels ascended and descended. The Lord confirmed the promised land and covenant. Jacob awoke, anointed the land, and named it Bethel.

22-28

GENESIS

discussion BYTES

Abraham knew God in such a way he fully trusted God's plan, even if it meant he was told to sacrifice his son. Can we say, without a doubt, that we have walked with God repeatedly and memorized what it felt like to trust Him? Where in our lives can we trust God more?

_____
_____
_____
_____

Jacob repeatedly gets caught up in scheming and cheating the system. Once habits are formed, it becomes challenging to get rid of them. What patterns in your life are causing harm? Or how did you break the habits that challenged you?

_____
_____
_____
_____

Esau sold his inheritance for a bowl of stew. Esau was so caught up in the moment of his desire he gave no thought to how that would affect his future. What inheritance have you sold because it wasn't what you desired at the moment, not worth it or needed? Or did you feel you didn't deserve the inheritance?

_____
_____
_____

PODCAST

22-28

GENESIS

How does your story connect now or in the past to Isaac, Rebekah, Esau or Jacob?

GENESIS 22-28

# REMIX

Our blessings come out of obedience...

"'AND ALL THE NATIONS OF THE EARTH WILL BE BLESSED BY YOUR OFFSPRING BECAUSE YOU HAVE OBEYED MY COMMAND.'"
Genesis 22:18

GENESIS 22-28

POST Credits

Father,

today I thank You for Your faithfulness, even when I didn't take the time to worship You in it. I submit my moments to You, not to my flesh. Every testimony I have should glorify You. I repent for not doing any of these things. I release the patterns that have me circling the drain and instead pick up what Your word has to say about my circumstances.

Amen

GENESIS 22-28

EPISODE 5
Trailer

Jacob was now on the run from a furious brother! He runs into the love he always longed for and finds safety in his uncle's home. However, deceit from someone else is on the horizon, and Jacob gets a dose of his own medicine. He runs straight into the arms of the wrong woman and has lots of kids with her, some other ladies, and the love of his life (Oh, brother!). After years of labor, he was humbled and worked towards some unification and healing of his relationship with his brother. He had a little trouble with his kids (don't we all) and had quite a few struggles on yet another life-changing journey.

29-35

GENESIS

29-35

GENESIS

PLUG IN

competitive HEARTS

We can grow weary in competing with others when we should just try to be a better version of ourselves.

Jacob went to Haran, seeking refuge from his brother's anger, and found sanctuary in the home of Laban, his mother's brother. He saw the servants in the field, and just like in a slow-motion scene in a romantic movie, Rachel came across the field. And Jacob WAS IN LOVE, just like his father. He even asked the servants to move out of the way.

> "He said, 'Behold, it is still high day; it is not time for the livestock to be gathered together. Water the sheep and go, pasture them.'" (29:7)

He likely hit the ground with a few push-ups to look ripped and then heroically moved the stone for Rachel's father's sheep to be watered. He then went in for the kiss, and Rachel "wept aloud." Fireworks went off in her heart. He told Rachel who he was, and she ran to tell her father. Her father, Laban, was also excited and brought Jacob to his home. He stayed with his kin for a month and served Laban. Laban told Jacob he couldn't work for free because they were related. Jacob responded that he would commit seven years of labor for Rachel's hand in marriage in exchange for payment. Laban agreed, and Jacob served his time. When his time was done, he asked for Rachel to be his wife. They celebrated, but Laban sent Leah, his other daughter, instead. Jacob didn't get the honeymoon he expected with Rachel. The deceiver was deceived. He woke to find it was Leah, and Laban explained it was customary to give the firstborn in marriage first. Laban wasn't wrong. This was true in their culture.

GENESIS 29-35

PLUG IN

competitive HEARTS

continued ...

Not exactly ecstatic, Jacob did complete the week of celebration of matrimony with Leah; though, he was still smitten with Rachel, so he agreed to another seven years of service for her hand in marriage. This family's generational curse followed them: the deceit of Rebekah, her brother Laban, and now her son Jacob. What a web of deceit and lies we can weave when controlled by the desires of our flesh.

The Battle of the Babies commenced. Leah believed the birth of her children would bring her love from Jacob. She had one son after another, totaling four, while continuously hoping Jacob would look at her as he did Rachel. The Lord graciously gave Leah children but not Rachel. It wasn't to spite Rachel but out of favor towards Leah for how she was treated.

Infertility can be such a hard trial to endure. Rachel's trial of infertility was perhaps met with a lot of questions—ones that can cause any couple to feel desperate for solutions. Yet, it can also cause some hard, irresponsibly placed blame on each other.

"When Rachel saw that she bore Jacob no children, she envied her sister. She said to Jacob, 'Give me children, or I shall die!' Jacob's anger was kindled against Rachel, and he said, 'Am I in the place of God, who has withheld from you the fruit of the womb?'"
(30:1-2)

Following in Grandma Sarah's footsteps, Rachel gave her servant to Jacob.

PLUG IN

competitive HEARTS

continued ...

The action caused a tug of war between Rachel & Leah as each offered up their servants and themselves for Jacob to have more children. Their desperation for time with Jacob even led to an exchange of fertility plants called mandrakes. At the end of the Battle of the Babies, Jacob ended up with twelve children: six sons and one daughter from Leah, one son from Rachel, and four sons from servants.

Many times, you will see the words, "God remembers." The Hebrew translation does not imply that the Lord has forgotten anything; rather, this would be the moment He should regard it. God remembering each of these ladies at specific times was all in His grand plan. It had nothing to do with forgetting them. Though I imagine it might have felt that way, it was not intended that way.

Everything is in His timing. Have you ever felt forgotten or that God has seemingly disregarded your situation? Don't give up hope in His faithfulness. Many stories end before God's ending. Let Him "remember" you when the timing is right. Whether you experience your own Battle of the Babies or get more than you can handle, don't get caught up in what the Lord has for someone else. Focus on the moments and gifts God intended for you.

GENESIS 29-35

PLUG IN

GIVE ME freedom

Humbled hearts, when we get a dose of our own medicine.

Jacob asked his uncle for freedom to leave for his homeland and take his wives and children with him. Laban recognized he had been blessed only through Jacob and wanted to give him a "going-away present." Jacob wanted nothing but to be able to take care of his family. He told Laban that if he could leave, he would pasture the flock and remove all the speckled, spotted, and black ones. Laban agreed but then deceitfully removed all the striped, spotted, and black ones and sent them with his sons. He left Jacob to pasture the rest of the flock. After recognizing the betrayal, Jacob set out to pasture the flock by setting up an elaborate stick breeding program that proved successful. Laban's sons were jealous. Jacob realized he should probably go, and the Lord confirmed. He called a family meeting and told his wives, "It is time to go; your daddy keeps cheating me, but my Lord keeps blessing me." Rachel and Leah became upset that their father left them with nothing but agreed to leave with Jacob.

They left for the land of Canaan, but not before Rachel took what she believed she rightfully deserved. When Laban discovered they had secretly exited, he pursued them. Laban had a dream that God told him to chill, and when Laban caught up with Jacob to question him on his actions, he played it off coyly. He wanted them to know he would have given them a proper send-off if given the option. God warned him but he still had something to say.

29-35
GENESIS

PLUG IN

GIVE ME freedom

continued ...

"And now you have gone away because you longed greatly for your father's house, but why did you steal my gods?'" (31:29-30)

Jacob confessed he feared Laban would have taken his family, but also, whoever amongst them was a thief would die. Unknowingly, Jacob's wife was the thief. Growing up in a family of deceivers, she must have learned a thing or two; she managed to wiggle her way out of the search and seize with the old period excuse. It worked, and Jacob was angry with Laban. He then word-vomited twenty years of pent-up feelings.

Laban compromised and asked for a covenant that they stay away from each other but requested Jacob would take care of his daughters. The deceit of Laban humbled Jacob, and his family continued their journey.

Anticipating a run-in with his brother, Jacob became nervous and decided to send a message ahead of him to Esau. Seeking favor, he offered his livestock and servants. When the messengers returned, they reported Esau was on his way with 400 men. Okay, stop there. 400, you say? That doesn't sound like a well-anticipated, joyful reunion. Rightfully scared, Jacob split his camp in two to increase the odds of survival and then prayed. Something very beautiful occurred in his prayer:

29-35 GENESIS

PLUG IN

GIVE ME freedom

continued ...

"And Jacob said, 'O God of my father Abraham and God of my father Isaac, O Lord who said me, 'Return to your country and to your kindred, that I may do you good,' I am not worthy of the least of all the deeds of steadfast love and all the faithfulness that you have shown to your servant, for with only my staff I crossed this Jordan, and now I have become two camps. Please deliver me from the hand of my brother, from the hand of Esau, for I fear him, that he may come and attack me, the mothers with the children.'" (32:9-11)

His prayer was gratitude for God's mercy and grace in Jacob's life. Despite all of Jacob's actions, God continued to bless him. Jacob was aware of what the Lord had done for him and asked for even more grace and mercy by praying for protection from harm.

We can't say we always get it right; our actions will never be enough to earn His grace and mercy, but He gives it anyway. We are lucky we can go to His throne for such requests. His request line is always open, and like our favorite radio station, our song will eventually be played.

29-35 GENESIS

PLUG IN

Unexpected REUNION

We anticipate responses, but when the hand of God is in it, expect a different response.

Jacob sent a peace offering of livestock presented in separate droves by his servants to soften Esau before he met up with Jacob. He took his wives and children across the stream that night, leaving him alone. Jacob relentlessly wrestled with a man until morning, not giving up, and the man touched Jacob's hip. His hip came out of the socket, but that didn't affect Jacob. He was determined to have the man bless him. This "man" was God. Jacob had just wrestled with God. Jacob's life until now was met with challenges of deceit against and from him. Regardless, he refused to give up and start back at ground zero. He knew the Lord and fought to keep Him. He then received a name change from Jacob to Israel. It also mentioned that the "sinew" was not eaten because of this event. The "sinew" of the thigh is the ligament or tendon, which imparts a great source of strength between the muscle and bone. It was where Jacob was struck with an injury that conveyed precisely the type of person he was . . . strong-willed. His determination to be blessed and his belief he would be was how he received his blessing. His faith and willingness to cling to God gave him the courage not to give up.

Have you ever watched a movie at the edge of your seat or anticipated a confrontation with someone you have transgressions with or against? In the waiting, if our minds are dictated by our emotions, our thoughts can easily spin out into a million different directions. I am sure this was how Jacob felt—a million thoughts entered his mind before the reunion with his brother.

GENESIS 29-35

PLUG IN

Unexpected REUNION

continued ...

Jacob saw Esau coming with 400 men. He panicked and divided his wives and children into two groups, putting the servants and children on the frontline, with Rachel and Joseph being last. Then, he bravely went before them all, bowing seven times until he was confronted face-to-face with his brother.

What happened next was unexpected. Esau ran to his brother, hugged him, kissed him, and cried. What a rejoicing moment of forgiveness! Jacob, still not convinced, introduced his family as servants for his brother. Esau told him, "Nonsense, I am good." (Talk about a transformation.) We could easily say that maybe Esau did have to fight for everything he had, as his father said he would. His journey through it was not explained. But as his father said, he would never be blessed until he let go of the bitterness. But really it isn't important how he got through his bitterness, just that he did.

Jacob insisted that Esau accept his present. He recognized God's blessings and the repentance he must make with his brother.

"Jacob said, 'No, please if I have found favor in your sight, then accept my present from my hand. For I have seen your face, which is like seeing the face of God, and you have accepted me. Please accept my blessing that is brought to you, because God has dealt graciously with me, and because I have enough.' Thus he urged him, and he took it." (33:10-11)

GENESIS 29-35

PLUG IN

Unexpected REUNION

continued ...

If you ever heard someone say, "You might be the only Jesus they ever see?", this is a perfect example of this statement. Esau could have, in his flesh, held on to the anger and bitterness he once had, but somehow, he had healed. (I would love to hear that testimony. I'm sure that would have been a bestseller.) Jacob also could have held on to pride and never humbly offered himself to Esau. Yet, they were healing, and Jacob saw God in it all! Where can we heal in our lives? Can we forgive and let go of someone's sin against us? Can we admit the sin we have committed against someone else and share love? Can we provide blessings instead of hatred towards others even if . . . ? (You fill in the blank here.)

Esau and Jacob overcame a lifetime of hurt to heal from something that didn't really even belong to them. Holding on to transgressions brought anger, fear, and bitterness. Holding on to the sin of others or ourselves doesn't put us in the place God wants us. He wants us to eat at His table, not make deals over a bowl of stew, and fear the outcome forever.

GENESIS 29-35

Esau invited Jacob on his journey home, yet Jacob asked for his group to rest, and he would be right behind him. Jacob then bought some land and built an altar. I am sure the relief of the whole situation was worth a little rest and a whole lot of praise!

PLUG IN

SHAME & Recourse

Shame to your family can come in many ways, but our actions are what we are held accountable for.

In our next chapter, we see one of Jacob's daughters endure something I pray no person ever experiences. Shechem took Dinah, the daughter of Leah and Jacob, and raped her. He claimed his love for her and told his father, Hamor, to go and get her as his wife. Jacob's sons marched in from the fields as Hamor arrived to speak to Jacob. Hamor pleaded with them and told them Shechem loved her and wanted her as a wife. Hamor further stated that the families should be united in many marriages between their sons and daughters of the city. He offered their land to live and whatever else they desired, for Shechem was smitten.

However, the brothers of Dinah were scheming. They asked that Shechem and all the village men be circumcised, and then they could dwell as one. Hamor and Shechem agreed in delight (oh boy, I don't think this will end well). Hamor and Shechem gave a persuasive speech to the city men, and they agreed to be circumcised.

The next day, while all the men were weak and sore, Simeon and Levi killed all of them and rescued Dinah. The rest of the brothers cleaned the city out. Not just of jewels, either. They took their livestock, children, and wives. Oh, this didn't make their father happy.

"Then Jacob said to Simeon and Levi, 'You have brought trouble on me by making me stink to the inhabitants of the land, the Canaanites and the Perizzites. My numbers are few, and if they gather themselves against me and attack me, I shall be destroyed, both I and my household.'" (34:30)

29-35 GENESIS

PLUG IN

SHAME & Recourse

continued ...

Their response,

"... 'Should he treat our sister like a prostitute?'" (34:31)

How often have we come up against someone else's sin only to sin back against them? Hard things come with hard choices. When our flesh rises to injustices, we want to return to the adage "eye for an eye." Yet, it is not us who should seek vengeance.

It doesn't mean we condone the sins against us, but it also shouldn't mean we sin against them. Have you faced a challenging situation where it was tough to resist making a hasty decision in response? Injustices are hard to witness. Most of the time, it causes our emotions to rise, and we want to do something about it, naturally. Our superhero syndrome goes into full gear, and we operate out of character. How we engage in situations of injustice can change the trajectory of our walk with Christ and someone else's. It's important to seek wisdom in our actions to avoid havoc.

GENESIS 29-35

All this distress had been wearisome on Jacob. Needing a fresh start, he packed up his family to make an altar where he reunited with Esau. On the journey, the Lord protected them, and fear fell upon the surrounding cities of Jacob and his sons. Umm, maybe because your sons plundered a city and killed all the men?

PLUG IN

SHAME & Recourse

continued ...

A few more life changes happened before the end of these chapters. The family built an altar, Rebekah's nurse died and was buried under an oak tree, and God, again, blessed Jacob and reconfirmed the covenant of his father, Isaac, and grandfather, Abraham. Along their journey, pregnant Rachel went into labor but died shortly after giving birth. Before she did, they named their son Benjamin. Since they were not near the land where their ancestors were buried, Rachel, unfortunately, was buried along their path to Ephrath. Jacob/Israel journeyed to Eder without the love of his life, yet he'd be favoring someone else soon. While in Eder, his son Reuben slept with his father's mistress (Oh, Reuben!). At the end of this chapter, the family tree is reviewed, and Isaac's journey and life end. He was then buried by Jacob and Esau.

29-35 GENESIS

discussion BYTES

Rachel struggled as she watched her sister have what she could not obtain. It can feel as though God has forgotten you when you face circumstances you can't seem to understand. What circumstances are you struggling to have patience with for an outcome? Or have you grown comfortable leaning into God's timing?

_____
_____
_____

Jacob's history of deceit left him anxious about his pending reunion with his brother. He sought forgiveness but feared that Esau's heart might still be hardened. Our healing starts with forgiveness. Who do we start with? Is there someone you need forgiveness from, need to forgive, or have forgiven? What happened in between the trauma and the forgiveness?

_____
_____
_____

PODCAST

29-35

GENESIS

Simeon & Levi thought they were doing what was best for their sister Dinah. The injustice done to her made them angry, and their response was tragic. What damage have you experienced that has been caused by your response or the response of another amid an injustice?

_____
_____
_____

YOUR story

How does your story connect now or in the past to Jacob, Rachel, Leah, Esau, Dinah or Simeon and Levi?

_____
_____
_____
_____
_____
_____
_____
_____
_____
_____
_____
_____
_____
_____
_____
_____
_____
_____

29-35 GENESIS

You are not forgotten...

29-35

GENESIS

"WHEN RACHEL SAW THAT SHE WAS NOT BEARING JACOB ANY CHILDREN, SHE ENVIED HER SISTER. 'GIVE ME SONS, OR I WILL DIE!' SHE SAID TO JACOB."
Genesis 30:1

POST Credits 🙌

Father,

let me never forget You will not leave me in the trenches of my dark circumstances. I remain faithful, believing my blessings will come, and I am encouraged by Your word in the process. My response to the sins of others or my own should come from a place of healing. Show me, Father, where I fall short and need to be humbled and where I need to forgive.

Amen

GENESIS 29-35

EPISODE 6
Trailer

Sibling rivalry gets out of hand once again, but this time it is with Jacob/Israel's sons. The brothers became so annoyed with Joseph that they sold him into slavery. Yet, the last laugh would be on them when they later find him right where Joseph's dreams said he would be. This story is woven by The Master Himself, turning dire circumstances into His glory. Unfortunately, Joseph's journey will not be a cute Strawberry Shortcake cartoon; it will be filled with jealous brothers, his master's shady wife, and a senile cupbearer. Sounds like the soap operas my granny used to watch. Thankfully, those were fiction!

36-42

GENESIS

GENESIS 36-42

PLUG IN

Wardrobe
MALFUNCTION

If only we were a little more humble.

GENESIS 36-42

What an adventure we have been on; lots of family fighting, discord, and food being thrown around. Sounds like my family's Thanksgiving dinner. We might be able to pick who sits at the kiddie table, but we can't always pick who gets placed in our family tree.

Like many other men at that time, Esau took many wives—one of them being Ishmael's daughter, Basemath. After his father's death, he took his crew to live in the mountains of Seir, ironically meaning "shaggy." Esau moved away from his brother, Jacob. The land could not support both families and livestock. The group of people later became known as the Edomites. Esau or Edom's genealogy seems unimportant, like many of the long lists of relatives described in the Bible. Yet, if we follow the branches closely, we can witness God's promises through the generations, where even generational curses might have begun, and why some are yoked to these sins. This chapter also described the line of Seir the Horite, who we later realize was from the line of Ham (Noah's cursed son).

Making sense of the line of Esau and his crew can be overwhelming, yet we can deduce that genealogy and your lineage (where you came from) were important at this time, which was why they mentioned it. There is some truth to that today, but thankfully, our lineage doesn't determine our outcome. It is where God is bringing us, not where He has taken us from, that determines our outcome.

PLUG IN

Wardrobe
MALFUNCTION

continued ...

    Let's return to the less confusing parts of this chapter with good ol' Jacob. Jacob was living in Canaan, and man, he was busy. Twelve sons are not what God has gifted me, and I wake up appreciating that daily. He knew my two were enough for me.

    Remember that special lady of Jacob's—yes, Rachel. It isn't too hard to believe that Jacob favored her sons. One of those sons was her eldest, Joseph. Joseph worked with the servant wives' sons tending sheep and tattling on them. His brothers began to resent him and take note of the care given to him by their father. Jacob/Israel adorned cocky Joseph with a robe of many colors, and the resentment grew. What about us? Have we had animosity toward another, which festered and grew as we saw blessings bestowed on them? Such blessings can cause us to idolize what they have instead of finding joy in what they have been given.

    Adding fuel to the fire, Joseph bragged about a dream where his brother's sheaves bowed to his sheaves of grain. Then he shared another dream of the sun, moon, and stars bowing as well. His brothers were angered that their favored brother would rule them. His father and brothers rebuked him. His brothers became angry and jealous, but his father stayed low-key and kept his feelings to himself.

    With all of this unspoken animosity, it likely wasn't the wisest decision of his father to send him to the field to pasture the flock with his brothers. His brothers plotted to kill him as they saw him in the distance.

GENESIS 36-42

PLUG IN

Wardrobe
MALFUNCTION

continued ...

GENESIS 36-42

They mocked him and devised a plan to get rid of him. They planned to throw him into one of the pits and make up an elaborate story of an animal devouring him. Yet, Reuben, Leah's oldest son, tried to talk some sense into his brothers.

"But when Reuben heard it, he rescued him out of their hands, saying, 'Let us not take his life.' And Reuben said to them, 'Shed no blood; throw him into this pit here in the wilderness, but do not lay a hand on him.' That he might rescue him out of their hand to restore him to his father." (37:21-22)

Instead of fulfilling their plot to kill, they ripped off Joseph's robe and threw him into the empty pit. They did not regard Joseph as they ate, and their brother was left with nothing. Their reaction to the personality of their brother caused a domino effect of consequences. In the distance, they saw a caravan of Ishmaelites on their way to Egypt. Remember who the Ishmaelites were? Ishmael was Abraham's first son with the servant Hagar. This caravan is the nation of their great uncle. A great nation was made from him as promised, yet as we continue to read the story, we see he would also be a part of the making of another great nation.

Joseph became a great example of the saying, "God knows your heart." God knows you are a sinner and that, as a sinner, there will be times you will behave and make choices out of flesh. These choices can determine the fate of yourself and others.

PLUG IN

Wardrobe Malfunction

continued ...

    Knowing you will make these choices, God sets a course in motion to change the outcome, always staying a step ahead of us.

    Judah, one of Leah's sons, suggested they sell him to the Ishmaelites. The Midianite traders, the Ishmaelites, bought Joseph for twenty shekels of silver ($6) and took Joseph to Egypt. When Reuben returned to find his brother was gone, he asked his siblings, "Where shall I go?" Reuben was the eldest, so he probably felt the responsibility fell on him to take care of them all. Now there would be no place he could hide from the potential of his father's fury.

    So, they tried to conceal their crime by ripping the coat and dipping it in goat blood. The generational curse of deceit arose once again. They then brought the coat as evidence of the tragic death of their brother to their father. Jacob identified the coat as Joseph's and was beyond comfort. He mourned for days as his children tried to comfort him but said,

"... 'No I shall go down to Sheol to my son, mourning.'..." (37:35)

    The loss of a child is profound, and though Jacob might have favored this child, it is still something no parent is prepared to experience.

GENESIS 36-42

PLUG IN

Wardrobe
MALFUNCTION

continued ...

    The word "Sheol" mentioned in this verse is translated as a place of still darkness which comes after death. I have not experienced this loss before; therefore, I will not pretend to try to understand it fully. Yet, after reading this translation, I can only imagine the grief described was exactly like this—a place of still darkness.

    It is quite scary to think Jacob was experiencing such darkness. What might seem like the final resting place of your soul as you grieve is not the final resting place of your loved one. We can only pray that is what can bring us comfort as we navigate through our grief, that we can pull ourselves out of "Sheol" and remember the eternal life we are given in His name. That joy and grief can co-exist. Though the death of Joseph might not have been real, his father's grief was.

36-42

GENESIS

PLUG IN

Dream A LITTLE DREAM

Lots of things are up for interpretation, but with God on the throne, the truth remains evident.

One of Jacob's sons, Judah, grew a tumultuous family tree. First, his son, Er, was seen as evil, and God put him to death. Judah then encouraged his second son, Onan, to take Er's wife, Tamar, as his own and to raise Er's children. Onan was unhappy with this arranged marriage proposal, so he creatively avoided impregnating Tamar. God was not happy with his choices and sentenced him to death too. Judah then asked Tamar to remain a widow in her father's house until Shelah, his youngest son, was older. Judah feared his son would die due to disobedience like his older brothers.

Judah's wife then died, so he ventured off his land to shear his sheep and mourn. Tamar noticed Shelah was grown and became angry that she was not given to him. She heard of Judah's trip to shear his sheep and decided to conceal herself and follow him. Judah, grief-stricken, thought she was a prostitute and made a deal with her to give her a goat, but she asked that he leave a pledge of his signet, cord, and staff as collateral. Judah agreed.

Judah sent the goat to her with a friend and asked that he take back the pledge items from the woman. Unfortunately, the man was unable to find the "prostitute." Months later, Judah received word that Tamar had been immoral and declared she must be burned to death. Then, in what would now be considered a social media pregnancy reveal disaster, Tamar called Judah out as the father with his pledge items.

Dream
A LITTLE DREAM

continued ...

"Then Judah identified them and said, 'She is more righteous than I, since I did not give her to my son Shelah.' And he did not know her again." (38:26)

Judah felt he deserved it, for he had not given Shelah as promised. Tamar ended up having twins. The midwife tied a scarlet thread to Zerah's hand, believing he would be the firstborn, but his brother, Perez, beat him to it. Sounds like a repeat birthing story of Judah's father.

The story now spins back to Joseph. Potiphar, an officer of the Pharaoh of Egypt, purchased Joseph. Despite the circumstances Joseph found himself in, the Lord blessed him. Many recognized the Lord favored Joseph, so he also found favor from others. He became the overseer in the house. Because Joseph was blessed, the Egyptian house was blessed. Joseph was put in charge of everything due to the blessings he received.

Joseph was a very handsome, successful man who caught the eye of the master's wife. She flirted with him, but he rejected her and said,

"'He is not greater in this house than I am, nor has he kept back anything from me except you, because you are his wife. How then can I do this great wickedness and sin against God?'" (39:9)

She continued her advances and garnered the garment he left behind as evidence. She accused him of trying to "lie" with her and then ran through the house to scream of his transgressions.

Dream
A LITTLE DREAM

continued ...

His master was outraged and threw him in prison. Here, Joseph was shown favor once again. The keeper of the prison, recognizing the Lord favored Joseph, put him in charge of all the prisoners. Joining him in prison was the king of Egypt's cupbearer and baker. Both had dreams and were recognizably troubled by them. Joseph inquired about their bah-ben (sad faces-for those non-cajun). The cupbearer shared his dream first.

"...'In my dream there was a vine before me, and on the vine there were three branches. As soon as it budded, its blossoms shot forth, and the clusters ripened into grapes. Pharaoh's cup was in my hand and I took the grapes and pressed them into Pharaoh's cup and placed the cup in Pharaoh's hand.'" (40:9-11)

Joseph told the cupbearer that Pharaoh would restore him to his position in three days. He asked that the cupbearer not forget him and mention him to Pharaoh. The baker then told his dream to Joseph.

"...'I also had a dream: there were three cake baskets on my head, and in the uppermost basket there were all sorts of baked food for Pharaoh, but the birds were eating it out of the basket on my head.'" (40:16-17)

He told the baker that in three days, he would be hung. Sure enough, three days later, on Pharaoh's birthday, he restored the cupbearer to his position and hung the baker. Yet, the cupbearer forgot to mention Joseph's name to the Pharaoh.

GENESIS 36-42

PLUG IN

Counting GRAIN

We can say: Don't count your chickens before they hatch, but when you have a dream interpreted, you count grain before the famine.

Two years passed, and Pharaoh had two dreams. In the first dream, he was standing by the Nile; seven healthy cows were eating the grass, then seven malnourished cows were eating the healthy cows. In the second dream, seven healthy ears of grain grew on one stalk, and seven unhealthy ones grew next to them and swallowed up the healthy ones. The Pharaoh was troubled by his dreams and searched for an interpreter. Finally, the cupbearer snapped out of his senior moment and remembered Joseph in prison. He explained to Pharaoh Joseph's skill for interpreting dreams. Pharaoh called for Joseph. Joseph cleaned himself up and presented himself to Pharaoh. Pharaoh asked for Joseph to interpret his dream.

"Joseph answered Pharaoh, 'It is not in me; God will give Pharaoh a favorable answer.'" (41:16)

Joseph's answer was humble. It is important for us not to take credit for what God does through us. It would be easy for us to take full credit for our abilities, but we have them only because of the Lord.

GENESIS 36-42

Pharaoh then explained both of his dreams to Joseph. Joseph told Pharaoh the number of healthy cows and ears of grain represented the seven years of blessings and good harvest for Egypt; the seven unhealthy cows and ears of grain represented the famine that would consume the land in the following years. The reason for the two dreams meant this was set by God and would happen soon.

PLUG IN

Counting GRAIN

continued ...

Joseph recommended that a wise and discerning man oversee the land of Egypt to take a fifth of the produce to store away in preparation for the famine. Pharaoh realized no one else was qualified for the job and hired Joseph to be in charge of the plan to help save Egypt. Pharaoh dressed Joseph for the part, paraded him around town, and changed his name to Zaphenath-Paneah. At thirty, Joseph married a priest's daughter, Asenath, and had two sons, Manasseh and Ephraim.

> "Joseph called the name of the firstborn Manasseh. 'For,' he said, 'God has made me forget all my hardship and all my father's house.' The name of the second he called Ephraim, 'For God has made me fruitful in the land of my affliction.'" (41:51-52)

I have always considered Joseph's outlook on life special. Though it might not be mentioned in the Bible, Joseph's emotions and actions didn't always paint the picture of unicorns and rainbows and line up with God's word. What an incredible reputation he must have had for his story to be told with such resilience and honor. He was representing Jesus before Jesus even walked the Earth. Can we say the same for our lives? What would our story look like if written by others?

For the seven years of abundance, Joseph stored grain. As predicted, seven years of famine followed, yet Egypt would be full of bread. The surrounding cities began to come to Joseph for grain. He opened the storehouses and began to sell the grain to the people.

GENESIS 36-42

PLUG IN

Counting GRAIN

continued ...

Meanwhile, Jacob heard of grain for sale in Egypt and told his sons, "What are you waiting on?" Stop fiddling around and get some. Way to whip those boys into shape, Jacob. Only ten of the brothers left for the journey. Can you guess which one doesn't go? Yes, the precious son of Rachel-Benjamin. Jacob feared something might happen to him, so he kept him home.

Joseph's brothers arrived in Egypt and bowed to the man in charge (as predicted by Joseph's dream), not knowing it was their brother. On the other hand, Joseph recognized them but treated them as strangers and accused them of being spies. They denied it and explained they were all the sons of one man seeking to buy food. Joseph continued his accusations as they tried to assure him they were not spies, and the youngest brother was home with their father. Joseph was relentless and said they would have to pass a test if they were not spies. The brothers must send one of them to bring the youngest brother back while the remainder are confined in Egypt.

For three days, the brothers were in the Pharaoh's custody. On the third day, Joseph approached them again with the proposal, yet changed the conditions. He asked that only one brother be left behind as the rest would be given grain for the family and be released to bring their youngest brother back to Egypt.

The brothers huddled in conversation, realizing they might have brought these circumstances on themselves for what they did to Joseph.

PLUG IN

Counting GRAIN

continued ...

Reuben said, "I told you not to sin against our brother, but did you listen–Nooooooo! Now we are paying for it." Joseph, eavesdropping with his interpreter, turned away and cried. He demanded Simeon stay behind. He filled their bags with grain but returned their money at the top of every sack. Mercy. Despite their actions, Joseph mercifully gave them something they did not deserve.

The brothers departed on their trip and discovered the money in their sack, making them very nervous. They made it home and explained the whole situation to Jacob. I imagine it sounded like my three kids running in all at once to tell me what happened that day—times three.

"And Jacob their father said to them, 'You have bereaved me of my children: Joseph is no more, and Simeon is no more, and now you would take Benjamin. All this has come against me.'" (42:36)

Forgetting all the times God had been there, Jacob was still heavily grieving. We can easily be outside a story and think c'mon, Jacob. But that is because we already know the ending of this story. Would we be just as reluctant as him if we didn't know the ending? Reuben then promised Jacob that he would kill his two sons if he did not bring Benjamin back. Jacob was not convinced, and his grief overcame him.

"But he said, 'My son shall not go down with you, for his brother is dead, and he is the only one left. If harm should happen to him on the journey that you are to make, you would bring down my gray hairs with sorrow to Sheol.'" (42:38)

discussion BYTES

Joseph's brothers were quite jealous of him, which festered into hatred. The animosity spiraled out of control as they watched Joseph prosper from blessings. As we experience hardship, it isn't easy watching others prosper. Are we harboring jealousy over the blessings bestowed on others, and how does it affect us daily?

_____
_____
_____
_____
_____
_____

Joseph could have easily been upset by the cupbearer's forgetfulness, but instead, when Joseph was finally pulled from prison, he helped anyway. Joseph's forgiveness was out of obedience to his gift from the Lord. He placed what the Lord set before him before his offense. In what ways has being offended kept you from continuing to use your gifts?

_____
_____
_____
_____

How does your story connect now or in the past to Jacob/Israel, Joseph, or his brothers?

_____
_____
_____
_____
_____
_____
_____
_____
_____
_____
_____
_____
_____
_____
_____
_____
_____
_____

REMIX

Letting go of pride for what is righteous...

GENESIS 36-42

"THEN JUDAH IDENTIFIED THEM AND SAID, 'SHE IS MORE RIGHTEOUS THAN I, SINCE I DID NOT GIVE HER TO MY SON SHELAH.'..."

Genesis 38:26

POST Credits

Father,

what an incredible plan You have orchestrated for me. I might not completely see the blueprint, but I trust Your promise. I am humbled by the gifts You have bestowed on me, and I will use them to glorify You. I will not forget where You are in my story and allow Your will to be done.

Amen

GENESIS 36-42

genesis
43-50

EPISODE 7
Trailer

There's some serious baggage to be unpacked in these last chapters. Joseph's family straightens up long enough to get a plan together to not starve just in time for a family reunion. Forgiveness is central to this story, and the healing that comes over the family is beautiful. It gives this family hope that the ending of their story will turn out better than the beginning. Even though that one time in the restaurant with your two-year-old proved unsuccessful after they flung mashed potatoes at the guests next to you, there is hope he will be a productive citizen someday. We close out the book of Genesis this week, leaving you, hopefully, stirring in your soul as you explore more of your own story in the pages God has written for you.

43-50

GENESIS

PLUG IN

MOTIVES IN *action*

We have often learned how desperate someone can become when hungry, but hunger isn't always the motive.

Joe's family ran out of the grain they were blessed with, and Jacob told them they must return. His sons reminded him of the warning they were given. They were not to return unless they brought Benjamin (Like, hello, y'all left Simeon for a really long time). Jacob/Israel was upset because he didn't want to lose another son. Judah, not ready to spare another brother, promised to protect Benjamin. After all, he was the brother who had the idea to sell Joseph.

> "And Judah said to Israel his father, 'Send the boy with me, and we will arise and go, that we may live and not die, both we and you and also our little ones. I will be a pledge of his safety. From my hand you shall require him. If I do not bring him back to you and set him before you, then let me bear the blame forever.'"
> (43:8-9)

Jacob agreed, sent some adorning gifts, doubled the money for grain to be given to the man (Joseph), and prayed for them. The brothers made their journey. When the brothers arrived, Joseph invited his brothers to eat, but not without the brothers shaking in their sandals with fear that they were still cursed. It was honorable that they were honest about the money in their first grain bags; however, it was for fear of what could happen to them, not for the sake of another. Sounds like their father after his deceit with his father. Simeon was released, and they were taken into Joseph's house to be catered to. As Joseph greeted them, they presented him with the gifts, and Joseph inquired about their father.

GENESIS 43-50

MOTIVES IN *action*

continued ...

    They answered, and then Joseph noticed Benjamin and was overcome by such emotion that he left the room to weep. I'm sure the glimpse of an older Benjamin caused a mix of emotions for Joseph.

    Joseph once again commanded his servant to fill the brothers' sack with grain and to place their money back on top. Yet, this time, he asked that his silver cup be placed in Benjamin's bag. After they left for their journey back home, Joseph sent his steward to follow them and accused them of thievery. They were shocked and began to argue they were incapable of such a thing. They even replied,

"Whichever of your servants is found with it shall die, and we also will be my lord's servants." (44:9)

    The cup was found in Benjamin's bag, and the brothers expressed their agony by tearing their clothes. Back in Egypt, they fell to the ground in front of Joseph. They pleaded to be cleared of the crime, yet Joseph had another plan. He wanted to see if his brothers had changed since his "death."

"But he said, 'Far be it from me that I should do so! Only the man in whose hand the cup was found shall be my servant. But as for you, go up in peace to your father.'" (44:17)

    Judah pleaded their case by describing the relationship of their elderly father and Benjamin, the only child left of his mother's children.

GENESIS 43-50

MOTIVES IN *action*

continued ...

Judah's compassionate story for his father was moving. His heart was where it should be. He didn't beg Joseph to reconsider for him but for his father. He even offered himself in place of Benjamin. Again, Joseph was overcome by emotion and asked that everyone leave the room except his brothers.

> "And Joseph said to his brother, 'I am Joseph! Is my father still alive?'..." (45:3)

Ummm, say what? His brothers were now stupidly staring. So Joseph began to explain who he was, showed them mercy, and said,

> "And now do not be distressed or angry with yourselves because you sold me here, for God sent me before you to preserve life." (45:5)

> "So it was not you who sent me here, but God. He has made me a father to Pharaoh, and lord of all his house and ruler over all the land of Egypt." (45:8)

GENESIS 43-50

God had grace, and Joseph showed mercy. He will go ahead of you to preserve His promise. The sooner we are obedient, the sooner His promise is fulfilled. In what areas of your life are you not being obedient? Could it be preventing you from the promise He has for you?

PLUG IN

joyful REUNION

Reunions come with mixed emotions, though overwhelming joy should be the greatest.

Joseph then asked his brothers to go and get their father, so they could all live happily ever after together. The joyful reunion of hugs and crying began, and Pharaoh heard of Joe's brothers in the house. He welcomed them with wealth and property. Joseph sent them back on their journey home to bring back their families. He showered his brother Benjamin more than his other brothers, yet he still loaded them all with provisions. And I love this: as Joseph sent them on his way, he said,

"... Do not quarrel on the way.'" (45:24)

In other words, y'all behave and don't sell any other brothers off to a slavery ring (Too soon?). So, the brothers brought their father the joyous news.

"But when they told him all the words of Joseph, which he had said to them, and when he saw the wagons that Joseph had sent to carry him, the spirit of their father Jacob revived." (45:27)

Pause for a bit. Can you imagine this? My heart wept here. Tears ran down my face. The death of a child, as we spoke about before, is the most heart-wrenching experience one could ever live through. But how much more joy would there be to find out they are alive and well? I believe this is what heaven will be like—a reunion that will last for eternity.

PLUG IN

joyful REUNION

continued ...

Jacob then had a dream, and God reassured him this was the correct path. He promised him a great nation and Joseph would be the one to close his eyes for his last breath. Joseph's family was now on their way to Egypt, coming in hot and loaded. Every member of their family—husbands, wives, and children. Did you read the entire list? It was seventy people! If you told me seventy family members were moving into town with me, I would say, "Peace out" (just kidding).

Since Judah couldn't just text his brother to meet them in Goshen, he went ahead of them to deliver the message himself. Joseph rode out to meet them; the reunion was an Instagrammable moment. Israel explained to Joseph he could die now, content and happy, knowing he was able to see him one last time. Joseph prepared his family to meet Pharaoh, for he was concerned about their well-being. Egyptians did not consider being a shepherd an honorable occupation.

To keep them safe, Joseph changed their titles to entice Pharaoh, livestock keepers. Yet, the brothers were honest with Pharaoh, and he honored them with honorable jobs. Jacob visited Pharaoh, they had a friendly conversation, and then Jacob blessed him.

Joseph was still responsible for caring for the land, and with the on-going famine, many villagers were starving. Villagers began to run out of money to buy grain, so Joseph asked for their livestock in exchange for food. After a year, the villagers were desperate to sell themselves and their land, so Joseph purchased it all for Pharaoh, the beginning of the 400 years of slavery.

GENESIS 43-50

PLUG IN

joyful REUNION

continued ...

Only the land of the priests was left alone. Joseph had a plan, though:

"Then Joseph said to the people, 'Behold, I have this day bought you and your land for Pharaoh. Now here is seed for you, and you shall sow the land.'" (47:23)

Their despair turned to hope as Joseph showed them a way out. They were fruitful and multiplied greatly. Jacob/Israel was now 147 and close to death. He made a request of Joseph: not to be buried in Egypt but to be buried with his fathers. Joseph assured him he would honor the request. Jacob had a heartfelt conversation with his son about his heartaches and joys, then met his grandsons, Manasseh & Ephraim.

"And Israel said to Joseph, 'I never expected to see your face; and behold, God, has let me see your offspring also.'" (48:11)

43-50
GENESIS

PLUG IN

EXPECTATIONS *not met*

Going into situations with preconceived notions might elude us from God's true path for us.

What an unexpected ending for Jacob. He thought he knew what his ending would be, but it was so different from what he expected. Have you had something turn out differently than anticipated and better than expected?

Jacob reminded them of the promise he was given by the Lord and placed his hands on Joseph's sons to bless them. Yet, Joseph realized his father put the wrong hand on the wrong firstborn and tried to switch it. Jacob informed him he knew what he was doing—back off, Joseph! Both would be great, but the younger would be greater—sound familiar? Jacob ended by telling them God would be with them and that someday, they would live in the land of their fathers. The rest of the sons gathered by their dying father's bedside, bid him goodbye, and took whatever blessings he had for them. Each of these tribes was called and blessed for a purpose much more significant than their tribe.

The Blessings of Jacob's sons:

GENESIS 43-50

† **Reuben** - Jacob was not happy with this son. I guess the first can be the last, and nothing comes from Reuben's tribe. His desire to be loved much like his mother and his uncontrolled passion for his father's slave proved to be a lifelong affliction faced by his entire family.

PLUG IN

EXPECTATIONS
not met

continued ...

✝ **Simeon & Levi** - If you remember correctly, these were the men who slayed all the men in the village for raping their sister. Simeon's tribe became the weakest one. Levi's tribe would serve an honorable purpose as priests, yet they would be given no land of their own. They were both stripped of any power to do anything of this magnitude ever again.

✝ **Judah** - He received the firstborn birthright and from his tribe would come Jesus! Jacob mentioned in his blessing that Judah was a lion's cub, and Jesus is referred to as the lion of Judah. The scepter not parting would mean the ruler's staff would never be taken away. The garments of wine represented Jesus' blood-stained clothes. All little nuggets leading to Jesus. When Judah was born, his mother, Leah, praised the Lord. Throughout his life, Judah showed his heart with his desire to protect his brothers and father and even his wayward sons, even if it meant a sacrifice of self. It was a well-suited blessing that his life would forever be victorious and lead to a man who made the greatest sacrifice for us.

43-50 GENESIS

PLUG IN

EXPECTATIONS
not met

continued ...

✝ **Zebulun** - His mother named him Zebulun because she said he brought her great honor. And so would his tribe. His blessing positioned his tribe in just the right place to help David's army later.

✝ **Issachar** - If you recall, this guy was conceived in exchange for some mandrakes. His tribe became a large tribe but a tribe of slaves. Enslaved by a deal!

✝ **Dan** - Sounds like a solid name for a judge, right? From his tribe came Samson. When Dan was born, Rachel desperately tried reworking God's plan through her slave. Dan's tribe was also desperate, calling out for salvation and redemption.

✝ **Gad** - His tribe was equipped to fight back, and they did. They were the troops in David's army. His birth, from Leah's servant, came with, as she said, "good fortune," so this tribe's success on the battlefield was birthed in him.

✝ **Asher** - His birth brought Leah great joy though he was not exactly hers. His blessing was not long, but he would be rich—Yay Asher!

GENESIS 43-50

EXPECTATIONS
not met

continued ...

- ✝ **Naphtali** - Another short and sweet one. His tribe was free-spirited, and I guess that is why Jesus began His teaching in their land; they were open-minded.

- ✝ **Joseph** - His tribe would always have God there, and blessings would always follow them. Jacob declared that God had turned it around despite what the enemy had planned for Joseph. From his tribe came Gideon, Joshua, and Deborah, all of whom delivered Israel from something.

- ✝ **Benjamin** - A fierce tribe that included King Saul and Paul. Their victories were selfish, but God still used them to accomplish His plan.

"All these are the twelve tribes of Israel. This is what their father said to them as he blessed them, blessing each with the blessing suitable to him." (49:28)

Jacob, again, requested to be buried with his fathers and took his last breath. Joseph embalmed his father, as was Egyptian tradition, and honored him for seventy days before he and his brothers buried their father as requested. After their father's death, his brothers began to worry Joseph's heart would not be so soft. Yet, Joseph felt differently,

"As for you, you meant evil against me, but God meant it for good, to bring it about that many people should be kept alive, as they are today." (50:20)

PLUG IN

Promise FULFILLED

Closing out the book doesn't mean we close your story.

There may be challenges in our lives that make it hard to be obedient, use wisdom, or seek love and forgiveness. But God orchestrates these times of challenge for a purpose that will fulfill His promise. If we focus on the challenges, we may never see the fulfillment of a promise through it. It doesn't mean something terrible has to happen to achieve His promise, but He will never give up on His promise for us. He will meet us where we are. No matter the circumstances, we should do the hard things and walk through them with God.

Joseph had quite a challenging life, yet in so many ways, he was blessed as well. He chose to look at those blessings and be reminded of what good God was doing in them. He pushed aside all that had been done against him to reach God's promise. Not only was he blessed through it, but others were also blessed. The villagers were kept alive, Egypt prospered, and his brothers were saved and given grace and mercy—all of these may not have happened had Joseph chosen to look at his circumstances differently. What circumstances in our life can we change our perspective on?

As we reach the end of the book of Genesis, the death of Joseph is a solemn reminder that God's promise lives on and doesn't die with him. His story is intertwined with the beginning of a story God has intentionally written for us. Our choices dictate us living out the story God mapped out for us. Our story is only the beginning of His story. There are many more generations of stories to come that will weave together

ONE beautiful story – God's love for us!

GENESIS 43-50

discussion BYTES

In what started out as a scary plot for Joseph, God pivoted and went ahead of Joseph to secure His promise. Our obedience to His word in our life will lead to His promise. In what areas of your life are you being disobedient? Could you be preventing yourself from the promise He has for you?

_____
_____
_____

Jacob's grief was immeasurable after the loss of his son, so any outcome bringing joy concerning his son Joseph was not expected. What have you anticipated that has turned out differently and/or better than you expected?

_____
_____
_____

Joseph had quite a challenging life, yet in so many ways, he was blessed as well. He chose to look at those blessings and be reminded of what good God was doing in them. He pushed aside all that had been done against him to reach God's promise. What circumstances in our life can we change our perspective to bring about the blessings God has in store for us?

_____
_____
_____

PODCAST

43-50

GENESIS

YOUR story

How does your story connect now or in the past to Jacob/Israel, Joseph or his brothers?

GENESIS 43-50

REMIX

Our circumstances become our testimonies...

43-50

GENESIS

"'AND NOW DO NOT BE DISTRESSED OR ANGRY WITH YOURSELVES BECAUSE YOU SOLD ME HERE, FOR GOD SENT ME BEFORE YOU TO PRESERVE LIFE.'"
Genesis 45:5

POST Credits

Father,

today I want to thank You for Your unfailing love even when I miss the entire point of Your plan. I pray for little reminders to be dropped around me when I forget Your grace and mercy. I pray for perseverance through the trials and for my focus to be on You, not my circumstances. I pray for my story to be led by YOU!

Amen

GENESIS 43-50

MICHELLE
Gautreaux

WRITER * SPEAKER * ILLUSTRATOR * ARTIST

Michelle was born and raised most of her life in southern Louisiana, which cultivated a love for storytelling. Her writing journey began at a young age, but it wasn't until she had children that she discovered the importance of telling those stories. However, it was her teaching, writing, and social work careers that deepened her compassion and understanding of God's people and their stories.

Eventually, she shifted her focus to helping others find their own stories by establishing a community Christian Art Center. In 2021, Hurricane Ida devastated her community, destroying the art center, and Michelle sought guidance from the Lord. She found solace in God's word and embarked on a new mission to help others discover their story in what remained through her latest Bible study series, Lost & Found.

Michelle lives with her husband in southern Louisiana and is navigating her new story as a mother with three adult children creating their own stories.

WEBSITE

INSTAGRAM

FACEBOOK

YOUTUBE

PODCAST